Compelling 5th edition challenges for CR1 to CR5

Traveling Encounters
Volume 1

Traveling Encounters
Volume 1

Written and Illustrated
by Jerry Joe Seltzer

email: Jerry@5thDnD.com

5thDnD.com is a free tool for DMs who want to inject some creative inspiration into their games.

- Randomly generate cities, villages, and taverns.
- Pull a descriptive NPC out of thin air!
- Is it locked or trapped? Don't vacillate. Generate!
- Add random twists and secondary objectives to your combat encounters.
- Critical failure? Blame the random generator for the consequences.
- Plus random treasure, magic item properties, and much more!

TABLE OF CONTENTS

INVOLVES A MERCHANT.

CAN BE USED IN A FOREST OR WOODED SETTING.

CAN BE USED IN A DRY OR DESERT SETTING.

TAKES PLACE IN MOUNTAINS OR HILLS.

INVOLVES A RIVER OR LAKE.

TAKES PLACE IN A VILLAGE SETTING.

TAKES PLACE IN A CITY SETTING.

USABLE IN A WINTER SETTING.

‡ SKILL AND TOOL PROFICIENCIES THAT ARE UTILIZED IN THE ENCOUNTER.

MIND THE GAP

SUMMARY: Kobolds catch the party in a tight spot.

CR1 225 xp
6 Kobolds

CR2 475 xp
10 Kobolds

CR3 600 xp
12 Kobolds

CR4 925 xp
15 Kobolds

CR5 2250 xp
30 Kobolds

READ TO THE PLAYERS

The road narrows to a tight crevice between two towering cliffsides. Ahead of you, blocking the passage is a merchant with a heavily-laden yak. The beast's great horns are so wide that they keep catching on the rocky walls. The merchant, a portly halfling man, is trying to coax the yak through, but with no success.

The merchant is named Jopp Tunley. He is friendly and cheerful, but getting frustrated with his enormous yak which he calls Mousy. The yak can get through if it will simply tilt its head at an angle and walk forward past the pinch point.

A WIS(animal handling) check DC 16 will succeed in guiding Mousy through the gap. Unfortunately, it is precisely at that moment when the kobolds attack.

COMBAT

Three kobolds, roused by the commotion, emerge loudly onto a ledge, 70 feet up on the right-hand cliff. They have slings in their hands and are squawking with enthusiasm, so happy are they to rain stones down upon these travelers.

The cliff walls are very rough and don't require a check to climb. However, if injured, a character will fall unless they make a STR(athletics) check DC equal to the damage sustained. Falling damage is 1d6 per 10 feet fallen (divided equally if fallen onto another character).

Kobolds who die will fall off the ledge. They may fall onto a character who is directly below them, inflicting 3d6 bludgeoning damage unless they make a DC 10 Dexterity saving throw.

Jopp Tunley takes cover underneath his yak. He has total cover there. If the yak has been maneuvered past the pinch point, it will move 10 feet forward per round. The yak has AC 15 and 65 hit points.

Round 1: The three kobolds fire their slings at random targets. Because of range, they fire at disadvantage. Then, more kobolds emerge. Up to six can fit on the ledge.

Round 2: The kobolds attack with their slings. There is another ledge 10 feet higher and 30 feet to the side of the first ledge. If the CR chart allows, that ledge also fills with kobolds.

Rounds 3+: Kobolds attack with their slings. If any characters are trying to scale the cliff, half of the attacks will be focused on them. As kobolds are killed, they are replaced by more kobolds, until there are no more.

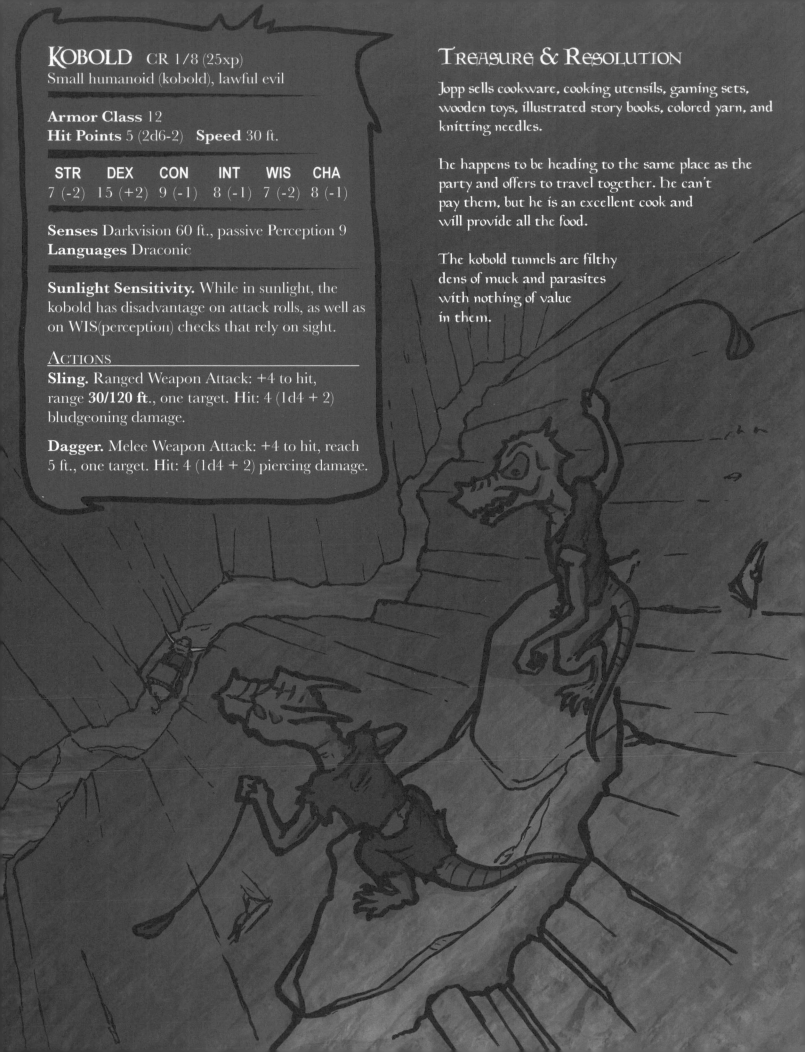

KOBOLD CR 1/8 (25xp)
Small humanoid (kobold), lawful evil

Armor Class 12
Hit Points 5 (2d6-2) **Speed** 30 ft.

STR	DEX	CON	INT	WIS	CHA
7 (-2)	15 (+2)	9 (-1)	8 (-1)	7 (-2)	8 (-1)

Senses Darkvision 60 ft., passive Perception 9
Languages Draconic

Sunlight Sensitivity. While in sunlight, the kobold has disadvantage on attack rolls, as well as on WIS(perception) checks that rely on sight.

ACTIONS
Sling. Ranged Weapon Attack: +4 to hit, range **30/120 ft.**, one target. Hit: 4 (1d4 + 2) bludgeoning damage.

Dagger. Melee Weapon Attack: +4 to hit, reach 5 ft., one target. Hit: 4 (1d4 + 2) piercing damage.

TREASURE & RESOLUTION

Jopp sells cookware, cooking utensils, gaming sets, wooden toys, illustrated story books, colored yarn, and knitting needles.

he happens to be heading to the same place as the party and offers to travel together. he can't pay them, but he is an excellent cook and will provide all the food.

The kobold tunnels are filthy dens of muck and parasites with nothing of value in them.

PITCHED BATTLE

SUMMARY: A clever use of music can give the players safe passage across a field of harmonic plants.

CR1 400 xp
2 Dire Wolves

CR2 600 xp
3 Dire Wolves

CR3 800 xp
4 Dire Wolves

CR4 1000 xp
5 Dire Wolves

CR5 1800 xp
9 Dire Wolves

READ TO THE PLAYERS

Your journey takes you through a vast, sunny field of waist-high flowering plants. Tubular stalks extend into the air like pan pipes, turning idle breezes into beautiful harmonies.

SKILL CHECK

If a character has proficiency in a musical instrument, they may make a WIS(musical instrument) check DC 12. If successful, they notice that their mere presence in the field is altering the pitch of the song. A clever predator with keen hearing could use this phenomenon to easily zero in on prey.

This means there could be predators already on the move while the party is caught in the middle of this expansive field. A challenging musical instrument check can be used to mask their presence. This is a CHA(musical instrument) check with a DC of 15. If this fails, the wolves will quickly hunt them down.

COMBAT

Dire wolves are large and, in the current environment, their stealth is worthless. A character with a passive perception of 12 or higher will spot the dire wolves when they are 100 feet away.

The wolves will close to attack. With their speed of 50, it should take them 2 rounds to get into melee.

Once in melee, the wolves will always attack in pairs or trios so that they can use their Pack Tactics feature.

On their turn, if any of the wolves have been killed AND they are currently outnumbered, the wolves will disengage and flee.

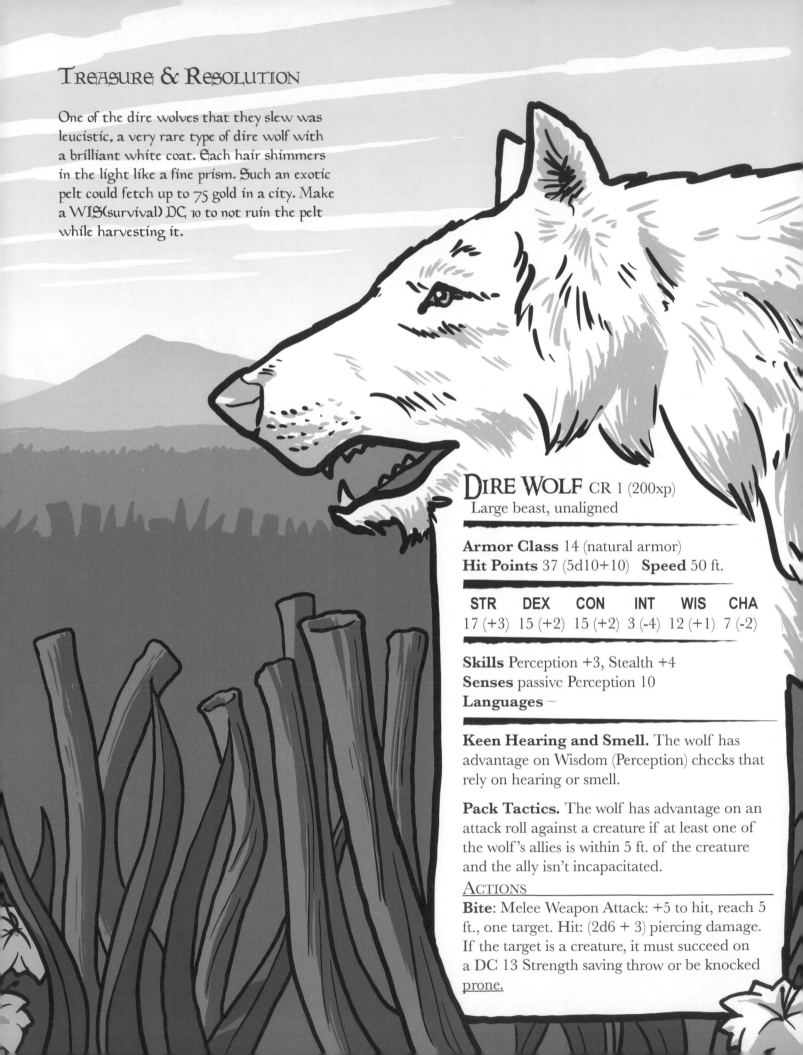

Treasure & Resolution

One of the dire wolves that they slew was leucistic, a very rare type of dire wolf with a brilliant white coat. Each hair shimmers in the light like a fine prism. Such an exotic pelt could fetch up to 75 gold in a city. Make a WIS(survival) DC 10 to not ruin the pelt while harvesting it.

DIRE WOLF CR 1 (200xp)
Large beast, unaligned

Armor Class 14 (natural armor)
Hit Points 37 (5d10+10) **Speed** 50 ft.

STR	DEX	CON	INT	WIS	CHA
17 (+3)	15 (+2)	15 (+2)	3 (-4)	12 (+1)	7 (-2)

Skills Perception +3, Stealth +4
Senses passive Perception 10
Languages –

Keen Hearing and Smell. The wolf has advantage on Wisdom (Perception) checks that rely on hearing or smell.

Pack Tactics. The wolf has advantage on an attack roll against a creature if at least one of the wolf's allies is within 5 ft. of the creature and the ally isn't incapacitated.

ACTIONS
Bite: Melee Weapon Attack: +5 to hit, reach 5 ft., one target. Hit: (2d6 + 3) piercing damage. If the target is a creature, it must succeed on a DC 13 Strength saving throw or be knocked prone.

Song for the Cabbage Farmer

Summary: 13-year-old Lamarra and her father, Rolf, were taking their load of cabbages to market, they were set upon by a small roving band of gnolls. The gnolls killed Rolf and also the donkey. Their appetites sated, the gnolls are now contemplating killing Lamarra just for fun. She began singing a soulful dirge to comfort herself and, luckily, the singing has entranced the gnolls. It has been over an hour now and her singing voice is starting to falter.

CR1 250 xp
2 Gnolls

CR2 450 xp
3 Gnolls

CR3 600 xp
4 Gnolls

CR4 975 xp
2 Gnolls
1 Gnoll Captain

CR5 2010 xp
7 Gnolls
1 Gnoll Captain

Read to the Players

A light breeze carries with it a sweet song from up ahead. As you slow your steps, the song becomes more clear. It is a soulful dirge sung to guide the dead into the afterlife.

Through the trees, a hundred feet up the winding trail, you spy the source of the song. A girl of perhaps 13 is standing atop a cart piled high with cabbages. She stands just out of reach of some gruesome gnolls surrounding the cart. A man lies dead on the ground along with the donkey that had been pulling the cart. Both man and donkey appear to be half-eaten.

The girl looks weary and her voice is beginning to falter. The song which has been keeping the gnolls entertained is beginning to lose its effect.

Combat Begins

Pre-initiative: Players could get a surprise attack before the gnolls spot them if their Stealth checks all exceed 10. Otherwise the gnolls notice them and combat begins.

Round 1: The gnolls are keen to use their Rampage ability. They will focus their attacks on the nearest one or two combatants in hopes of taking them down quickly.

Round 2: The gnolls continue to focus their attacks on just one or two player characters.

Mid-Battle Twist

Round 3: If she is still alive, Lamarra slips and falls. She rolls out the back of the cart along with dozens of round cabbages, creating a 10x15ft area of difficult terrain. Beginning a turn in this area or entering this area requires a DC10 DEX(acrobatics) check to prevent falling down prone.

Round 4: Lamarra will get up and flee from the fight, assuming she makes her DEX(acrobatics) check. She will draw the attention of the closest gnoll who will try to kill her, abandoning whatever scuffle he was already engaged in. Lamarra has an AC of 11 and 5 hitpoints.

Rounds 5+: The gnolls will continue to fight to the death, focusing their attacks on just one or two combatants if possible.

Treasure & Resolution

Each gnoll had a wooden shield and a spear. Their hide armors are smelly and infested with parasites. One of the spears is of elven design and beautifully crafted. The spear is not magic but a DC15 INT(investigation) check will reveal that the haft can be unlocked and the spear folded in half for easy storage. It has a value of roughly 8 gold.

The donkey cart is in good condition and can be pulled or pushed by two people or one very strong person. Rolf has a coin pouch with 12 silver and 8 copper. Lamarra has 1 silver and 3 copper in a pocket sewn into her dress.

If Lamarra has survived the encounter, she is very distraught. Her family lives an hour's walk from here in a small village called Joxenpatch. If the PCs return Lamarra and her father's body to the village, the villagers will thank them with food, beds, supplies, and information about what lays ahead on their journey.

GNOLL CR 1/2 (100xp)

Medium humanoid (gnoll), chaotic evil

Armor Class 15 (Hide Armor, Shield)
Hit Points 22 (5d8)   **Speed** 30 ft.

STR	DEX	CON	INT	WIS	CHA
14 (+2)	12 (+1)	11 (+0)	6 (-2)	10 (+0)	7 (-2)

Senses Darkvision 60 ft., passive Perception 10
Languages Gnoll

Rampage. When the gnoll reduces a creature to 0 hit points with a melee attack on its turn, the gnoll can take a bonus action to move up to half its speed and make a bite attack.

ACTIONS

Bite. Melee Weapon Attack: +4 to hit, reach 5 ft., one creature. Hit: 4 (1d4 + 2) piercing damage.

Spear. Melee or Ranged Weapon Attack: +4 to hit, reach 5 ft. or range 20/60 ft., one target. Hit: 5 (1d6 + 2) piercing damage

GNOLL CAPTAIN CR 2 (450xp)

Medium humanoid (gnoll), chaotic evil

Armor Class 16 (Hide Armor, Shield)
Hit Points 44 (8d8+8)   Speed 30 ft.

STR	DEX	CON	INT	WIS	CHA
17 (+3)	15 (+2)	12 (+1)	8 (-1)	11 (+0)	10 (+0)

Senses Darkvision 60 Ft., passive Perception 10
Languages Goblin

Rampage. When the gnoll reduces a creature to 0 hit points with a melee attack on its turn, the gnoll can take a bonus action to move up to half its speed and make a bite attack.

ACTIONS

Multiattack: This gnoll can make two attacks with its spear.

Bite. Melee Weapon Attack: +4 to hit, reach 5 ft., one creature. Hit: 4 (1d4 + 2) piercing damage.

Spear. Melee or Ranged Weapon Attack: +4 to hit, reach 5 ft. or range 20/60 ft., one target. Hit: 5 (1d6 + 2) piercing damage

SURVIVE THE AVALANCHE

SUMMARY: Caught in an avalanche, each character must struggle to survive.

READ TO THE PLAYERS

You are heading down a white hillside, deeply packed with snow. Suddenly, and without warning, the whole snowy face of the hill breaks loose, sweeping you downhill. You are caught in a life or death situation!

CR1
200 xp
d4

CR2
400 xp
d6

CR3
600 xp
d8

CR4
800 xp
d10

CR5
1000 xp
d12

HOW IT WORKS

Each player will make a series of checks. They will accumulate dice based on their check results. At the end, they will roll their dice to find out how buried they are, and can then dig themselves out. Everything happens very fast. There is no time to talk or plan amongst themselves. They may take a single reaction. Feather Fall gives them advantage on all their subsequent Acrobatics and Athletics checks.

WIS(survival) or INT(nature) DC 12

They know to steer their body (or their mount) towards the side of the flow.

ROLL DEX(ACROBATICS) DC12

OR IF MOUNTED:
WIS(ANIMAL HANDLING) DC15
ON A FAILURE THEY ARE DISMOUNTED

Give the player two dice (see CR for dice type)

They must try to swim against the flow to keep from being buried. If they were mounted they are swept off their mount.

ROLL STR(ATHLETICS) DC12

Give the player one dice (see CR for dice type). They make one more check, angling their body to stay atop the flow.

ROLL DEX(ACROBATICS) DC12

OR IF MOUNTED:
WIS(ANIMAL HANDLING) DC15
ON A FAILURE THEY ARE DISMOUNTED

Give the player one more dice.

They get one last check to swim towards the surface.

ROLL STR(ATHLETICS) DC12

Give the player two more dice.

They get one last check to fight their way up through the snow.

ROLL STR(ATHLETICS) DC12

Give the player one final die.

Give the player two final dice.

Give the player three final dice.

RESOLUTION

The hillside, now cleared of much of its snow, reveals an entrance. Perhaps this is a place integral to the plot of the campaign. Maybe it is the entrance to a dungeon. Or it could just be the lair of a formidable monster trying to hibernate through the winter.

BURIED ALIVE!

Each player should roll their dice and total them up. This number represents how many feet of snow is on top of them when the avalanche ends.

ROUND BY ROUND ACTIONS

The weight of the snow makes it hard to cast spells. **To cast a spell** they must make a concentration check (which is a Constitution saving throw) DC10 + 1 for every 5 feet of snow above them.

The cold, pressure, and lack of air combine to cause 1d4 hit point damage each round. If a character drops to zero hitpoints they automatically fail a death save each round thereafter. In this unique situation, the normal suffocation rules are suspended.

On each round a buried character can spend their action to make a STR(athletics) check with <u>disadvantage</u>. The check result is how many feet they climb towards the surface.

A character who reaches the surface may make a WIS(perception) check to listen for a buried ally. The DC equals the depth of the closest ally. Once they locate a buried ally they can then dig down towards them, as an action, at the rate of 1d4(+STR mod) feet per round.

Mounts should all emerge from the snow safely after a few rounds, though at half hit points.

Moon Shadow Emergence

SUMMARY: An eclipse turns day to night and unveils an eternal battle between the undead.

READ TO THE PLAYERS

You are traveling across the Dead Hills where armies clashed and died for thousands of years for reasons long forgotten. A shepherd grazing his flock nods to you solemnly as you pass. Each of you knows to be gone from these hills before the sun sets. The bright sunlight thankfully keeps the restless souls here locked away during the day.

The hills stretch for only a few miles yet the journey seems to take forever. You notice the sky begin to change color. The whispers of tormented spirits start scratching at the doorways to your minds. The dying scream of the shepherd, now far behind you, pushes you even faster to flee this area, but it is too late. The sun is becoming nothing but a dark hole in an inky blue sky. A cold wind catches up to you and then suddenly there are hundreds of figures blocking your path, acting out all the battles of the past.

You are trapped inside a thick, crushing sea of ghostly warriors fighting unending skirmishes. Thankfully, this eclipse should only last a couple minutes and most of the spirits seem to be ignoring you. Except for *that* one! That one warrior with a spear dispatches his opponent then wheels around to attack you!

CR1 400 xp
2 Spectral Soldiers

CR2 600 xp
3 Spectral Soldiers

CR3 800 xp
4 Spectral Soldiers

CR4 1000 xp
5 Spectral Soldiers

CR5 1800 xp
9 Spectral Soldiers

SPECIAL CONDITIONS

There is a dense crush of people battling around the PCs. Visibility is limited to 10 feet. Movement is extremely difficult. A DEX(acrobatics) or STR(athletics) check must be made as an action to move any distance. The distance moved is a number of feet times the check result.

INT(religion) DC 15 will reveal that the eclipse should only last about 2 minutes (20 ROUNDS). After that the sun will reemerge and these undead will vanish again until nightfall.

Expect players to get creative and allow them some liberty. This scenario is not well addressed by the standard rules, so be flexible.

COMBAT

The spearman has noticed them and engaged them in combat. He will continue his attacks until he has been vanquished.

Any time a player misses an attack, their mishap draws the attention of another spectral soldier who then engages them in combat. This continues until the maximum number of spectral soldiers has engaged them (based on the CR of the encounter.)

If there is still time left in the encounter and no soldiers are attacking, have one more soldier take notice of them. Again, the maximum that will engage them over the course of the entire twenty rounds is the number listed in the CR.

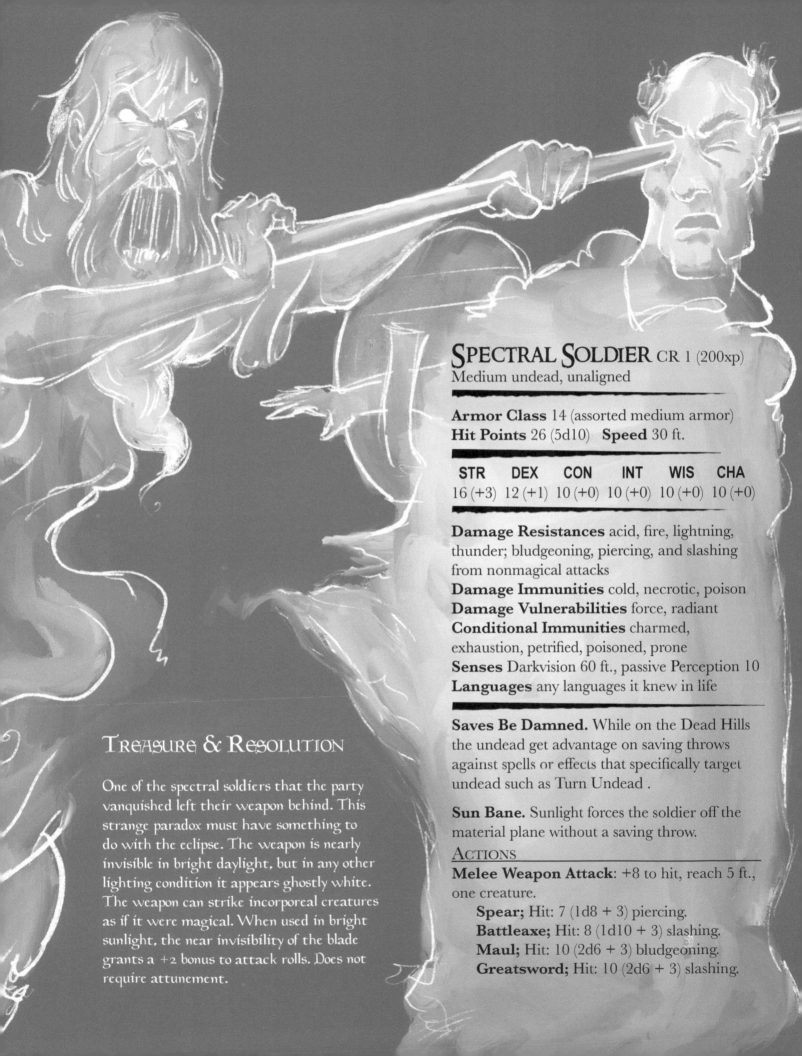

Treasure & Resolution

One of the spectral soldiers that the party vanquished left their weapon behind. This strange paradox must have something to do with the eclipse. The weapon is nearly invisible in bright daylight, but in any other lighting condition it appears ghostly white. The weapon can strike incorporeal creatures as if it were magical. When used in bright sunlight, the near invisibility of the blade grants a +2 bonus to attack rolls. Does not require attunement.

SPECTRAL SOLDIER CR 1 (200xp)
Medium undead, unaligned

Armor Class 14 (assorted medium armor)
Hit Points 26 (5d10) **Speed** 30 ft.

STR	DEX	CON	INT	WIS	CHA
16 (+3)	12 (+1)	10 (+0)	10 (+0)	10 (+0)	10 (+0)

Damage Resistances acid, fire, lightning, thunder; bludgeoning, piercing, and slashing from nonmagical attacks
Damage Immunities cold, necrotic, poison
Damage Vulnerabilities force, radiant
Conditional Immunities charmed, exhaustion, petrified, poisoned, prone
Senses Darkvision 60 ft., passive Perception 10
Languages any languages it knew in life

Saves Be Damned. While on the Dead Hills the undead get advantage on saving throws against spells or effects that specifically target undead such as Turn Undead .

Sun Bane. Sunlight forces the soldier off the material plane without a saving throw.

ACTIONS

Melee Weapon Attack: +8 to hit, reach 5 ft., one creature.

    Spear; Hit: 7 (1d8 + 3) piercing.
    Battleaxe; Hit: 8 (1d10 + 3) slashing.
    Maul; Hit: 10 (2d6 + 3) bludgeoning.
    Greatsword; Hit: 10 (2d6 + 3) slashing.

DARK ICE REFLECTION

SUMMARY: Fey attack the party in the guise of their own reflections.

CR1 400 xp
1 Winter Nixie per PC

CR2 600 xp
1 Winter Nixie per PC

CR3 800 xp
1 Winter Nixie per PC

CR4 1000 xp
1 Winter Nixie per PC

CR5 1800 xp
1 Winter Nixie per PC

READ TO THE PLAYERS

The water extends before you, iced over and dusted with snow. Animal tracks in the powder serve as proof that the ice is safe to travel on. So, you set off.

Halfway across, a stiff wind arrives and blows the snow aside. The ice below your feet is dark and smooth and suddenly very slippery. Your reflections stare back up at you with unsettling glares. Each of you watch your reflections draw your favorite weapon and immediately strike up at you through the ice!

SPECIAL CONDITIONS

Despite the illusion that the nixies are deep in the ice, they are actually right at the surface. INT(arcana) DC 20 is needed to reveal this obscure information.

The ice is very smooth and slippery in thanks to the influence of the nixies presence beneath their feet. Moving of any kind, including standing up, requires a DEX(acrobatics) check DC 12. Failure results in the character falling prone. A prone character has disadvantage on attack rolls and their nixie has advantage on attack rolls against them.

The PCs are striking down at their feet. A critical fumble is likely to strike their own feet or legs, or at least cause them to slip and fall prone.

WINTER NIXIE
Medium fey, chaotic evil

Armor Class 16 (natural armor)
Hit Points (same as PC they are imitating)
Speed (always located beneath PC as long as they are on the ice)

STR	DEX	CON	INT	WIS	CHA
14 (+2)	14 (+2)	12 (+1)	12 (+1)	12 (+1)	13 (+1)

Skills Perception +4, Stealth +5
Damage Immunities Cold
Senses Darkvision 60 Ft., passive Perception 14
Languages Sylvan

Magic Resistance. The winter nixie has advantage on saving throws against spells and other magical effects.

ACTIONS
Weapon. Melee or Ranged Weapon Attack: +(4+CR) to hit, one creature. Hit: 1d6 + CR piercing damage. Regardless of the nature of the weapon, it emerges from the surface as a sharp spike of ice.

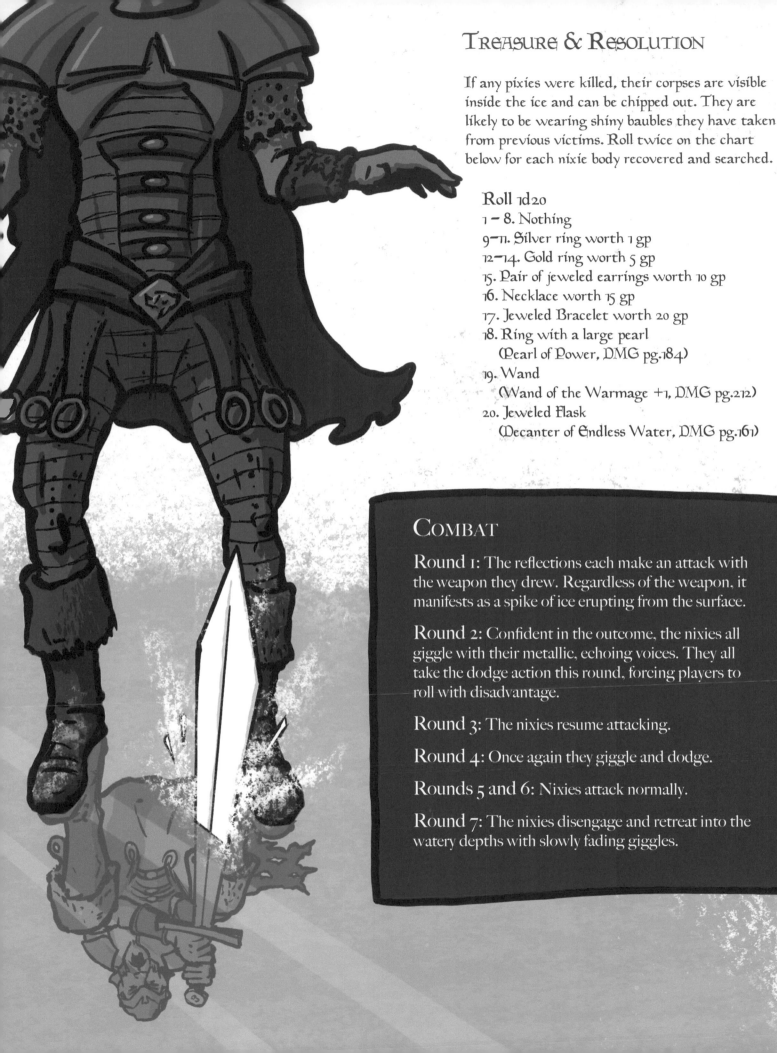

Treasure & Resolution

If any pixies were killed, their corpses are visible inside the ice and can be chipped out. They are likely to be wearing shiny baubles they have taken from previous victims. Roll twice on the chart below for each nixie body recovered and searched.

Roll 1d20
1 – 8. Nothing
9–11. Silver ring worth 1 gp
12–14. Gold ring worth 5 gp
15. Pair of jeweled earrings worth 10 gp
16. Necklace worth 15 gp
17. Jeweled Bracelet worth 20 gp
18. Ring with a large pearl
     (Pearl of Power, DMG pg.184)
19. Wand
     (Wand of the Warmage +1, DMG pg.212)
20. Jeweled Flask
     (Decanter of Endless Water, DMG pg.161)

Combat

Round 1: The reflections each make an attack with the weapon they drew. Regardless of the weapon, it manifests as a spike of ice erupting from the surface.

Round 2: Confident in the outcome, the nixies all giggle with their metallic, echoing voices. They all take the dodge action this round, forcing players to roll with disadvantage.

Round 3: The nixies resume attacking.

Round 4: Once again they giggle and dodge.

Rounds 5 and 6: Nixies attack normally.

Round 7: The nixies disengage and retreat into the watery depths with slowly fading giggles.

DRAGON FALL

SUMMARY: A mother dragon crashes to the ground dead while carrying her clutch of hatchlings.

CR1 400 xp
2 Hatchlings

CR2 600 xp
3 Hatchlings

CR3 800 xp
4 Hatchlings

CR4 1000 xp
5 Hatchlings

CR5 1800 xp
9 Hatchlings

READ TO THE PLAYERS

You hear a sound in the distance, like two great beasts fighting. Crashes, roars, and screams appear to be coming from the sky but you see only clouds. Then suddenly, two distant shapes far above, emerge from the cloud, one clearly fleeing from the other. Dragons! The pursuer tears the wing off the other, the final blow. As the injured one plummets to the ground, faster and faster, you get a sense of how massive these two dragons are. The victor flies away, apparently satisfied. The other crashes into the ground. A debris cloud marks the spot, a mere mile or so away from you.

COMBAT

Round 1: One hatchling uses their acidic breath weapon. All others go for bite attacks.

Round 2: A different hatchling uses their breath weapon, trying to catch two party members in the line if possible. The others continue their bite attacks.

Round 3: One of the hatchlings who has been wounded will disengage and retreat back into mamma's mouth. Roll a d6 for each of the others. On a 1-4 they bite, on a 5 or 6 they breathe acid.

Round 4: An enormous yellow cloud of acidic vapor escapes from the mother dragon's mouth and fills a 30 ft radius area 10 feet high. It is part of the death process of the dragon. Anyone who starts their turn in the cloud takes 2d4 acid damage and must make a Con save DC 15 or be blinded. They may make a new save each round until their sight returns.

Rounds 5+: Repeat Round 3. The cloud dissipates on round 7.

WHAT THEY WILL FIND

The female adult black dragon is dead. She was transporting a clutch of hatchlings in her mouth wherein they were protected from both the battle and the subsequent fall. As the players examine the fallen dragon, the mouth eases open. The hatchlings, scared and hungry, will climb out and begin attacking.

Treasure & Resolution

There are no clues as to where this black dragon came from nor why it was pursued and killed by the other one. Clearly, it was moving its hatchlings to a new location, but for what reason remains a mystery.

The various bits of dragon are the treasure. A good rule of thumb is that every pound of dragon can be traded for 2 gold, regardless of which bits they take.

If they manage to capture any living hatchlings, you can enjoy showing them what a manipulative, cunning, chaotic-evil dragon is capable of.

Black Dragon Hatchling

Medium dragon, chaotic evil   CR 1 (200xp)

Armor Class 16 (natural armor)
Hit Points 22 (4d8+4)   Speed 30 ft., swim 30 ft.

STR	DEX	CON	INT	WIS	CHA
13 (+1)	14 (+2)	12 (+1)	8 (-1)	10 (+0)	13 (+1)

Saving Throws Dex +4, Con +3, Wis +2, Cha +3
Skills Perception +4, Stealth +4
Damage Immunities Acid
Senses Blindsight 10 ft., Darkvision 60 Ft., passive Perception 14
Languages Draconic (understand but not speak)

Amphibious. The dragon can breathe in air and water.

Actions

Bite. Melee Weapon Attack: +4 to hit, reach 5 ft., one creature. Hit: 4 (1d6 + 1) piercing damage plus 2 (1d4) acid damage

Acid Breath (Recharge 5-6). The dragon exhales acid in a 10 foot line. Each creature in that line must make a DC 11 Dexterity saving throw, taking 13 (3d8) acid damage on a failed save, or half as much on a successful one.

CHAOS IN A CANDLE

SUMMARY: An acolyte grabbed the wrong candle for his master's candelabra and magma mephits are set loose in the temple.

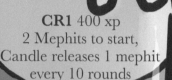

CR1 400 xp
2 Mephits to start,
Candle releases 1 mephit
every 10 rounds

CR2 600 xp
3 Mephits to start,
Candle releases 1 mephit
every 5 rounds

CR3 800 xp
4 Mephits to start,
Candle releases 1 mephit
every 3 rounds

CR4 1000 xp
5 Mephits to start,
Candle releases 1 mephit
every 2 rounds

CR5 1800 xp
6 Mephits to start,
Candle releases 1 mephit
every round

READ TO THE PLAYERS

People start yelling, Fire!. You see the smoke coming from the temple. Folks from the community drop what they were doing and rush to form a bucket chain between the well and the temple.

High-pitched screeches emanate from within.

IF THEY ENTER THE TEMPLE READ THIS:

A priest and a young acolyte are inside, trying to fend off fiery flying imps while also tamping out the fires the imps keep sparking. A black candle sits in a stand on a table, burning brightly and spewing sparks. Then it suddenly flashes and shoots another imp into the air as if fired from a musket.

Roll Initiative.

What are those things?

INT(arcana) DC 14: Those things that look like fiery imps are magma mephits. They are elementals who are vulnerable to cold, and they explode when killed.

OBJECTIVES

Extinguish Candle: Putting out the candle will stop more mephits from emerging. It is no harder to extinguish than a normal candle would be.

Save The Temple: When they enter the temple there are three small fires. One round of actions by a character should be able to extinguish one small fire. Mephit breath weapons and death bursts may spark new fires. Give the temple a general saving throw DC 10 when these things occur.

Defend The Men: The priest and the acolyte will not flee from the temple. They continue to put out fires and endure attacks by the mephits. Each starts with 20 hitpoints and AC 10.

COMBAT

Round 1: The mephits each choose a random target to attack with their claws. One of them uses their breath weapon and will try to catch at least two people in their cone of fire. Be sure to track the rounds and add new mephits as the candle burns down (refer to the CR chart).

Round 2: One mephit uses their breath weapon. Another casts Heat Metal (PHB pg.250) on a PC's armor or, if none are wearing medium or heavy metal armor, upon a steel shield or sword instead. All other mephits make claw attacks.

Round 3: Allow any mephits who haven't used their breath weapon to do so now. The rest make claw attacks. After the mephits' turn, a man runs in with a bucket of water and dowses one of the fires.

Round 4: Another mephit casts Heat Metal if there is a good target. Others make claw attacks. A woman runs in with a bucket of water and the previous person runs back out. The priest casts a 1d8+3 healing spell on someone in need.

Rounds 5+: One mephit will escape out the door while the rest make claw attacks. Townsfolk continue to come in and out with buckets of water.

MAGMA MEPHIT   CR 1/2 (100xp)
Small elemental, neutral evil

Armor Class 11
Hit Points 22 (5d6+5) Speed 30 ft., fly 30 ft.

STR	DEX	CON	INT	WIS	CHA
8 (-1)	12 (+1)	12 (+1)	7 (-2)	10 (+0)	10 (+0)

Skills Stealth +3
Damage Vulnerabilities cold
Damage Immunities fire, poison
Condition Immunities poisoned
Senses Darkvision 90 Ft., passive Perception 10
Languages Ignan, Terran

Death burst. When the mephit reaches 0 hit points, it explodes in a burst of lava. Each creature within 5 feet of it must make a DC 11 Dexterity saving throw, taking 7 (2d6) fire damage on a failed save, or half as much damage on a successful one.

Innate spellcasting (1/day). The mephit can innately cast heat metal (spell save DC 10), requiring no material components. Its innate spellcasting ability is Charisma.

ACTIONS

Claws. Melee weapon attack: +3 to hit, reach 5 ft., one creature. Hit: 3 (1d4 + 1) slashing damage plus 2 (1d4) fire damage.

Fire breath (Recharge 6). The mephit exhales a 15-foot cone of fire. Each creature in that area must make a DC 11 Dexterity saving throw, taking 7 (2d6) fire damage on a failed save, or half as much damage on a successful one.

TREASURE & RESOLUTION

If the priest survives he gives the PCs the mephit candle as a gift (assuming the candle was put out.) INT(arcana) DC 15 to read the marks on the candle and determine how many mephits are still inside. An Identify spell will also work. Regardless of how many mephits were released from the candle, there are a number of mephits equal to the encounter CR still trapped inside.

CLAY OX CALAMITY

SUMMARY: A peddler using a clay golem ox to pull her wagon needs help when the ox goes berserk.

CR1 400 xp
Ox hitpoints: 20
Max. hitpoints: 45

CR2 600 xp
Ox hitpoints: 25
Max. hitpoints: 55

CR3 800 xp
Ox hitpoints: 30
Max. hitpoints: 65

CR4 1000 xp
Ox hitpoints: 35
Max. hitpoints: 80

CR5 1800 xp
Ox hitpoints: 50
Max. hitpoints: 105

READ TO THE PLAYERS

You hear wagon wheels turning and the sound of hooves but the pattern is wrong. The hoof falls don't sound right. Then, from over the hill in front of you, a wagon appears. It is being pulled by one very large and very fast ox. It is a peddler's cart, loaded down with all manner of wares. A young woman is fighting against the straps of the ox's harness, trying to get it under control.

"Help!" she cries out and then frantically points towards the rear of her wagon. "Get the jars!"

But now, upon seeing you, the strange beast lowers its massive horns and charges you!

What is that?

INT(arcana) DC 13: That ox is a clay golem. If damaged, clay golems can go berserk. But if fully healed, using acid, it will stop its rampage. It can't be hurt by nonmagical weapons.

COMBAT & OBJECTIVES

The ox will make a ram attack against the closest PC, if possible, every round until it is either fully destroyed or fully healed.

Kiseema, the peddler, will scream at them not to attack the ox, but to get the jars of acid and smash them on it. She has everything invested in this ox.

The acid is kept in a wooden compartment accessible from the rear of the wagon. The compartment contains 12 ceramic jars, each the size of a softball and packed in straw. A DEX(acrobatics) check DC 12 is needed to throw open the lid of the compartment and grab a jar. Remember, the wagon is moving violently. On a 1, they drop the jar and take 1d4 splash damage.

A character who has a jar of acid in hand at the start of their turn can attempt to hit the ox with it. Kiseema will yell to 'target his legs.' They must make a ranged attack. (Simple weapon, Thrown, range 20/50)

  AC 15+: the jar strikes the legs, shatters, and heals the ox for 2d6 hit points.
  AC 10-14: the jar strikes the ox's body, shatters, and heals the ox for 1d6 hit points.
  AC 8-9: the jar hits the ox but bounces off and doesn't shatter. It can be picked up again.
  AC 1-7: the jar missed the ox, hits the wagon and deals 2d6 damage to the wagon. If the wagon takes 15 damage, the ox breaks free from its yoke and gains a +4 bonus to its attack rolls.

TREASURE & RESOLUTION

The clay ox is two hundred years old. It tends to develop cracks especially in the legs and, if not maintained with acid, slowly accumulates damage. Kiseema, the peddler, just bought the ox a month ago. She was given the jars of acid but wasn't clear on how often to use them. She waited too long.

  If the party destroys the ox, Kiseema is furious at them. But, if they healed the ox with the acid, she is grateful and lets each of them choose a free item from her wagon. She has every item from the Adventuring Gear table (PhB pg.150) that is 50 gp or less.

BERZERK CLAY OX
Large construct, unaligned   CR 6 (2300xp)

Armor Class 14 (natural armor)
Hit Points (refer to CR chart)   Speed 30 ft.

STR	DEX	CON	INT	WIS	CHA
21 (+5)	10 (+0)	18 (+5)	3 (-4)	8 (-1)	1 (-5)

Damage Immunities acid, poison, psychic; bludgeoning, piercing, and slashing from nonmagical attacks that aren't adamantine.
Condition Immunities charmed, exhaustion, frightened, paralyzed, petrified, poisoned.
Senses Darkvision 90 Ft., passive Perception 9
Languages understands only a few commands.

Berserk. The golem becomes berserk if it drops below half hit points. The golem attacks the nearest creature it can see. If it cannot see a creature it will attack an object or structure. It becomes calm if it is restored to its full hit points.

Acid Absorption. The golem is not damaged by acid but healed by it instead.

Immutable Form. The golem is immune to any spell that would alter its form.

Magic Resistance. The golem has advantage on saving throws against spells and other magic.

ACTIONS

Ram. Melee Weapon Attack: +6 to hit, reach 5 ft., one creature. Hit: 9 (1d8 + 5) bludgeoning.

WHAT'S THE DEAL?

SUMMARY: The shopkeeper cannot sell the players what they want because it is locked away and he lost the key.

READ TO THE PLAYERS

"Can't help you," replies the old shopkeeper.

"Yes you can!" injects a teenage girl from across the room. She was polishing the wares but now comes over to the old man and waving a finger in his face. "You have exactly what they need. It's in the big trunk and you know it!"

"Can't open the big trunk," he says. "So, I can't help them."

"Please excuse my grandfather," says the girl. "He's not as sharp as he used to be."

"Never been sharp. Mostly known for my bluntness which is why I'm telling you I can't open the trunk."

"He lost the key," the girl says to you. "On purpose!"

"Not true. Don't listen to her. I *hid* the key on purpose," the old shopkeeper says. "Then, entirely on *accident*, I forgot the hiding place."

"You look like resourceful folks," says the girl. "Anything you can do to help?"

CR1 225 xp
2 Crawler Larva

CR2 375 xp
4 Crawler Larva

CR3 450 xp
6 Crawler Lara

CR4 875 xp
9 Crawler Larva

CR5 1850 xp
14 Crawler Larva

THREE SOLUTIONS

Knock: A Knock spell will quickly solve this dilemma.

Pick: The trunk has an ordinary, yet quality, lock built into it. It can be picked using Thieves Tools (DC 15). Each failed attempt represents ten minutes of trying.

Find: The key is hidden in the shop. INT(investigation) DC 20. Each failed attempt represents a half hour of searching. The key is in book. The shopkeeper had used it as a bookmark but hasn't picked up the book in a while.

Surprise! Combat

Round 1 (surprise round): No check is offered to avoid the surprise but some characters may have abilities that apply.

    As soon as the trunk is opened, wriggling white worms Spring Attack whomever is closest. They look like giant maggots, two feet long.

Round 2: Guided by smell, they will generally attack whomever is closest, but will be especially drawn to a PC who is known to smell strongly.

Rounds 3+: Mindlessly driven to feed, the larva will attack until killed.

What are these things?

INT(nature) DC 14: These are the larval form of Carrion Crawlers (MM pg.37). Some eggs must have stowed away in one of the items stored in the trunk.

Crawler Larva CR 1/4 (50xp)
Tiny monstrosity, unaligned

Armor Class 14
Hit Points 15 (2d10+4)   Speed 20 ft., Jump 50ft.

STR	DEX	CON	INT	WIS	CHA
8 (-1)	18 (+4)	14(+2)	6 (-2)	13 (+1)	4 (-3)

Skills Perception +5, Stealth +6
Senses passive Perception 15
Languages --

Actions

Bite. Melee Weapon Attack: +4 to hit, reach 5 ft., one creature. Hit: 4 (2d4 - 1) piercing damage.

Spring Attack. Crawler Larva can jump up to 40 feet away and make a bite attack. Due to their lack of visual senses this attack is made with disadvantage but, if it hits, it deals double damage.

Treasure & Resolution

The contents of the trunk depend on what the party was shopping for and what this shopkeeper specializes in. The carrion crawler larva have eaten every scrap of organic material in the trunk which would include some potion stoppers, leather armor, straps to metal armors, scabbards, belts, boots, books, scrolls, wands, staves, clothes, etc. If the item they were shopping for survived they are only charged half price, or they are charged half price for a different item.

TREE HUGGING TRAGEDY

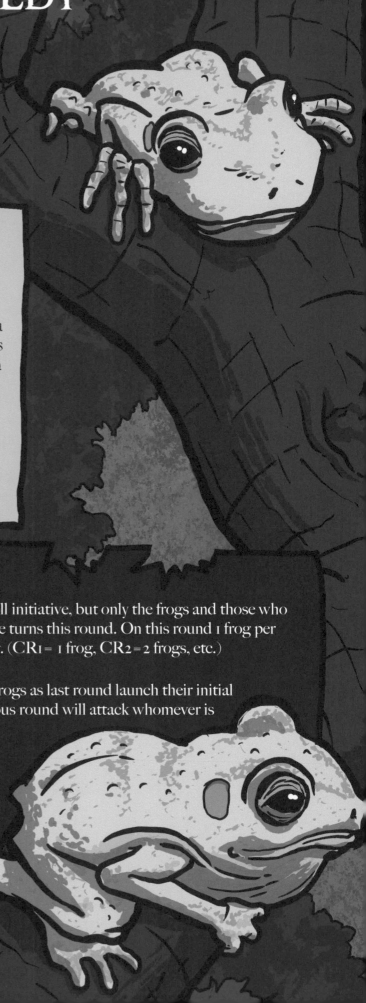

SUMMARY: Follia the dryad had enchanted a pair of giant tree frogs and also a passing paladin. Over time, the giant tree frogs multiplied and consumed all the animals in the area. The paladin, unable to part from his mistress, eventually starved to death and was fed upon by the frogs. Now the frogs are ravenous and Follia feels obligated to help feed them.

READ TO THE PLAYERS

While passing a stand of large, robust trees, you see the remains of a knight sprawled across the roots. His flesh has been picked clean. His chain mail armor is pushed up to his chest, revealing a skeleton devoid of anything other than the tracks left by gnawing teeth. His sword sits undrawn in its scabbard, as does his dagger.

Roll a Nature check DC15. Those who succeed realize the teeth marks look to be from giant tree frogs. Whereas everyone else is surprised when yellow frogs the size of leopards leap at you from the branches above.

COMBAT BEGINS

Round 1 (surprise round): Roll initiative, but only the frogs and those who made their Nature checks can take turns this round. On this round 1 frog per CR attacks at a random character. (CR1 = 1 frog, CR2 = 2 frogs, etc.)

Round 2: The same number of frogs as last round launch their initial attacks. The frogs from the previous round will attack whomever is closest to them.

Round 3: Any remaining frogs, according to the CR chart, launch their initial attacks. The rest continue to bite at their closest target.

CR1 225 xp
2 Giant Tree Frogs

CR2 375 xp
4 Giant Tree Frogs

CR3 450 xp
6 Giant Tree Frogs

CR4 875 xp
9 Giant Tree Frogs

CR5 1850 xp
14 Giant Tree Frogs

GIANT TREE FROG CR 1/4 (50xp)
Medium beast, unaligned

Armor Class 11
Hit Points 22 (4d8+4) Speed 30 ft., swim 30 ft.

STR	DEX	CON	INT	WIS	CHA
12 (+1)	13 (+1)	12(+1)	2 (-4)	10 (+0)	3 (-4)

Skills Perception +4, Stealth +5
Senses Darkvision 30 Ft., passive Perception 14
Languages –

Leaper. The frog can jump as far and as high as its speed (30). When assessing falling damage, the frog ignores the first 60 ft.

ACTIONS

Bite. Melee Weapon Attack: +3 to hit, reach 5 ft., one creature. Hit: 4 (1d6 + 1) piercing damage, and the target must also make a Con save DC 11 or take 2 (1d4) Poison damage.

MID-BATTLE TWIST

Round 4: The dryad, observing all this from within her tree, feels torn. She does not want to harm these innocent travelers but she also wants to give her frogs a fighting chance. She decides to cast Entangle and then let things play out.

ENTANGLE: Plants instantly grow up in a 20x20 area grabbing at people which makes them restrained. A Strength saving throw DC 14 means the character rips free and can ignore the entanglement. The giant tree frogs have advantage on their save against this spell.

RESTRAINED CREATURES have a speed of zero and have disadvantage on their attack rolls. Opponents gain advantage to attacks against them. Each round they can choose to use their action to attempt a DC14 Strength saving throw to free themselves.

Rounds 5+: The frogs will continue to attack until they are all dead or the party is. They are ravenous and will continue to bite any party members who drop (which inflicts one failed death save per bite). The dryad, still concealed, does not participate any further.

TREASURE & RESOLUTION

Upon the death of the last frog, the dryad's personal tree visibly darkens and shakes in sorrow. Leaves rain down upon the bones of the paladin.

Attempts to speak to the dryad go unanswered. If they attack her tree, she will retaliate (see Monsters Manual page 121.)

The paladin's possessions include chain mail armor, a shield, a longsword, and a dagger, a holy symbol, and a purse with gold coins in it. It contains 1d10 x the CR gold pieces.

BATHING BANDITS

SUMMARY: Tired of their own stink, a gang of outlaws has resolved to wash off the grime in a warm, bubbling spring. They are caught naked and unarmed.

CR1 300 xp
5 Outlaws

CR2 600 xp
8 Outlaws

CR3 1100 xp
11 Outlaws

CR4 1400 xp
14 Outlaws

CR5 2500 xp
20 Outlaws

READ TO THE PLAYERS

Lured by the joyful sound of men and women laughing together, you stumble upon a bathing scene. This rough-looking group has been relaxing in a warm, bubbling spring.

To your left, forty feet from the spring, their clothing is drip-drying on a makeshift clothesline strung between the trees. Their belts, holding dagger sheathes, dangle from low branches.

"Cripes!" shouts one of the women. "Bounty hunters!"

You realize instantly that this naked group is a band of murderous outlaws and you stand between them and their weapons.

AVOIDING VIOLENCE

Fast words may diffuse the situation. A WIS(insight) check of 12 will reveal that the outlaws will happily murder the PCs for their equipment regardless if they are bounty hunters or not. However, the outlaws are at a clear disadvantage here and can be convinced to let the PCs depart peacefully with a DC16 CHA(persuasion) check.

Combat

Round 1: The outlaws climb out of the pool and get to their feet on the mossy ground.

Rounds 2,3,4: Being unarmed, there are three options for the outlaws.
    A - Take the PCs' weapons. Make disarm attacks, and then their allies can pick up the weapons that are dropped. NOTE: Each outlaw can only attempt the disarm maneuver once.
    B - Get to their own weapons which are 40 feet away. They cannot get there and also grab a weapon in a single round.
    C - Grapple a PC and wrestle them into the pool.

Round 5+: If the fight is going well for the outlaws, they will continue to fight to the end. One or two of them may stop fighting to bandage fallen friends.

However, if the fight is even or in the PCs' favor, the outlaws will surrender and hope to escape later.

Treasure & Resolution

Each of the outlaws had leather armor and there are an equal number of daggers. Leaning against a tree are a quarterstaff, a rapier, and a shortsword. Coin pouches tied to belts contain 1d20 gold and 1d20 silver each.

Nearby, in an old iron mine, concealed by overgrowth and artful camouflage, is the outlaw hideout (Investigation DC, 13). Within the hideout are various bedrolls, blankets, and other sundry items. Notable among them are a half empty cask of wine, 2d4 crossbows (a mix of hand, light, and heavy), a friendly and affectionate tabby cat, 2d6 torches, and enough food for 2 days of rations for the PCs.

Hidden deeper in the mine (Investigation DC, 16) is a stash of stolen religious art such figurines, chalices, and ceremonial tools. They can be worth up to 200 gold to the right buyer but they are clearly stolen.

Bathing Outlaw CR 1/4 (50xp)

Medium humanoid (human), chaotic neutral

Armor Class 11
Hit Points 7 (2d6) **Speed** 20 ft. currently

STR	DEX	CON	INT	WIS	CHA
14 (+2)	12 (+1)	11 (+0)	10 (+0)	9 (-1)	10 (+0)

Skills Athletics +4
Senses passive Perception 10
Languages Common

Pack Tactics. The outlaw has advantage on melee attacks (including disarm attacks) when an ally is within 5 ft. of the target creature.

Disarm 1/day. +4 to hit vs. target's STR(athletics) or DEX(acrobatics) check. On a success, target's weapon lands in a random adjacent space. NOTE: Defender gains a +4 to their check if they are using two hands on the weapon.

Actions

Grapple. Athletics (+4) vs. target's STR(athletics) or DEX(acrobatics) check. On a success, the target gains the Grappled condition.

Melee Weapon Attacks. +4 to hit, reach 5 ft., one target. Normal weapon damage +2.

Ranged Weapon Attacks. +3 to hit, one target. Normal weapon damage +1.

BORN OF RECKLESS RESEARCH

SUMMARY: Seventy years ago the wizard Clarder The Undaunted was researching a powerful potion of animation in his tower. The unstable brew exploded with such force that it blew the top half of the stone tower apart. An iron box containing spell scrolls was coated in the magical concoction and subsequently buried in the remains of the tower. The box and the scrolls were steeped in the magic and eventually became animated. The box has been fighting its way to the surface for decades. Both it and the scrolls within are viciously angry.

READ TO THE PLAYERS

A rhythmic thumping draws your attention to the ruins of a wizard's tower set back from the road. The top half of the stone tower lay broken into heavy stone fragments at the base. Vibrantly colored ferns sprout from between the stones and from the top of the remaining tower. You can see that these ruins are many decades old.

The thumping noise is coming from a single wide stone that shifts up and down with each thump. The stone looks to weigh about fifty pounds.

ARCANA CHECK DC 20:
You think this tower belonged to Clarder The Undaunted, a wizard you recall was obsessed with animating objects.

CR1 260 xp
Animated Box
Scroll A

CR2 375 xp
Animated Box
Scroll A & Scroll B

CR3 525 xp
Animated Box
Scrolls A,B, & C

CR4 825 xp
Animated Box
Scrolls A,B,C,D,E

CR5 1310 xp
Animated Box
Scrolls A,B,C,D,E,F

COMBAT

Pre-Initiative: As soon as the stone is lifted or shifted, the iron scroll box will break free and the scroll(s) will leap out. Note that the uneven stones make for Difficult Terrain, doubling the cost of movement, but does not affect the animated objects.

Round 1: The box will bite at the legs of whomever is closest, if it can reach them with its 10 ft movement speed. Scroll A will cast Scorching Ray. Other scrolls will attempt grapple attacks. They will not attack someone who is already grappled by a scroll.

Round 2: Scrolls B and C will cast their spells on this round if they are not currently grappling someone.

Round 3: Any scroll that has not cast its spell will do so on this round if not currently grappling someone. If scroll D casts Darkness, it will give a huge advantage to the animated objects whom all have Blindsight.

Rounds 4+: The animated objects will continue their attacks until they are destroyed.

Treasure & Resolution

Unless they were attacked with any kind of fire or energy magic, the scrolls can be repaired using a Mending spell. They are then usable as normal scrolls. The iron box is battered and useless.

The wizard's tower had been looted long ago and been stripped bare. Though if they are willing to excavate the heavy stones at the base of the tower they will find a variety of crushed silver fixtures worth a total of 5 gold to a silversmith.

ANIMATED BOX CR 1/4 (450xp)

Small construct, chaotic neutral

Armor Class 16 (natural armor)
Hit Points 27 (5d8+5) **Speed** 10 ft.

STR	DEX	CON	INT	WIS	CHA
12 (+1)	14 (+2)	13 (+1)	2 (-4)	6 (-2)	1 (-5)

Damage Immunities poison, psychic
Conditional Immunities blinded, charmed, deafened, frightened, paralyzed, petrified, poisoned
Senses Blindsight 20 Ft., passive Perception 7
Languages

Antimagic Susceptibility.
(see Animated Scroll for description)

ACTIONS

Bite. Melee Weapon Attack: +3 to hit, reach 5 ft., one creature. Hit: 3 (1d4+1) bludgeoning damage.

ANIMATED SCROLL CR 1/2 (100xp)

Small construct, chaotic neutral

Armor Class 13
Hit Points 17 (5d6) **Speed** 40 ft.

STR	DEX	CON	INT	WIS	CHA
14 (+2)	16 (+3)	11 (+0)	8 (-1)	6 (-2)	1 (-5)

Damage Immunities poison, psychic
Damage Vulnerabilities fire
Conditional Immunities blinded, charmed, deafened, frightened, paralyzed, petrified, poisoned
Senses blindsight 60 ft. (blind beyond this radius), passive Perception 8
Languages –

Single Spell. Each scroll has 1 spell written upon it. The animated scroll can cast this spell once per day. It cannot cast its spell while grappling. Each scroll has a different spell.

Scroll A: Scorching Ray
Scroll B: Blindness
Scroll C: Mage Armor
Scroll D: Darkness
Scroll E: Mirror Image
Scroll F: Witch Bolt

Damage Transfer. While it is grappling a creature, the scroll takes only half damage dealt to it, and the creature grappled by the scroll takes the other half.

Antimagic Susceptibility. The scroll is incapacitated while in the area of an *antimagic field*. If targeted by *dispel magic*, the scroll must succeed on a Constitution saving throw against the caster's DC or fall unconscious for 1 minute.

ACTIONS

Grapple. Melee Weapon Attack: +4 to hit, reach 5 ft., one medium or smaller creature. *Hit:* The creature is grappled (escape DC 12). Until this grapple ends, the target is restrained and blinded. In addition, at the start of each of the target's turns, the target takes 7 (2d4+2) slashing damage.

FAVOR OF FATHER FROST

SUMMARY: Three priests of Telchur, god of winter, are transporting a holy relic to an important religious site. These powerful men have little patience for the miscreants blocking their path.

CR1 - CR5 400 xp
3 Priests of Telchur

READ TO THE PLAYERS

Suddenly, from behind, three men ride up on you on warhorses. They are wearing heavy armor and bluish-green cloaks trimmed with fine fur. These are clearly powerful men of faith to whom you pose no threat whatsoever. Attacking these men would mean certain death. Even the fear of disrespecting them sends shivers down your spines.

"Stand aside!" shouts the man on the lead horse.

"Not so fast, Balder," calls the second. "If you recall, the prophecy said the relic would cross paths with two groups on its journey. One group worthy of blessings and one group worthy of the Father's wrath."

"Which be you, then?" asks the lead rider. "Do you deserve rebuke or reward?"

RESPONDING TO THE PRIESTS

The party gets one chance at a CHA(persuasion) check. Before making that check, however, an INT(religion) check will determine how much of a bonus they will get due to their knowledge of this faith.

Step 1: Have each player roll INT(religion). Read each passage below that is equal to or less than their best check result.

DC 10+ (+2 bonus to persuasion check)
The priests are carrying the symbols of Telchur, god of winter, cold and the north wind. They are transporting a relic, a holy artifact, probably to perform a seasonal ritual at one of Telchur's temples.

DC 13+ (Total +4 bonus to persuasion check)
Telchur's followers seek to placate him more than worship him. He is revered by farmers and others who depend on the land's bounty, as well as those seeking relief from winter's chill.

DC 16+ (Total +6 bonus to persuasion check)
The cold northern wind shrouds all, draining life from man and beast alike, blowing out the flames of hope, leaving naught but infinite white silence.

DC 19+ (Total +8 bonus to persuasion check)
Telchurian priests pray just after darkness falls. Their duties include officiating at winter funerals, aid the fit in surviving the roughest parts of winter, and travel to spread the Ice Brother's gloom to distant peoples.

Step 2: Have the party decide who will speak for them. That character gains a bonus to their CHA(persuasion) check, as noted above.

Step 3: The priests judge the party in one of two ways, based upon the persuasion check result.

If the persuasion check is less than 14, the lead priest uses the relic on them. They are all made mute, unable to vocalize any sound at all. Each day at dawn they get to make a Wisdom saving throw (DC 15) to break the curse.
"Your words are like the babbling brook searching for the sea! Enough with you!"

If the persuasion check is 14 or higher, the lead priest hands out 5 potions of healing and 2 spell scrolls (Shield of Faith, Silence).
"Praise be to the Walker of the Wastes! Here, take these gifts in celebration of the Master of the North Wind. Blessings upon your travels."

PRIEST OF TELCHUR CR 6 (2300xp)

Medium humanoid, chaotic neutral

Armor Class 16 (Chainmail Armor)
Hit Points 65 (10d8+20)   **Speed** 30 ft.

STR	DEX	CON	INT	WIS	CHA
12 (+1)	11 (+0)	14 (+2)	14 (+2)	16 (+3)	12 (+1)

Senses passive Perception 15
Languages Common, Elven, Dwarven

Divine Strike. 2/day melee attacks can deal additional 1d8 cold damage.

Spellcasting. The priest is a 10th-level cleric. His spellcasting ability is Wisdom (spell save DC 15, to hit with spell attacks +7). The priest's preferred spells are **bolded**.

Cantrips (at will): Produce Flame, Sacred Flame, Resistance, Guidance, Spare the Dying,

1st level (4 slots): Inflict Wounds, Create or Destroy Water, Ray of Sickness, Command, **Shield of Faith**, Cure Wounds,

2nd level (3 slots): Calm Emotions, Lesser Restoration, Hold Person, **Silence**

3rd level (3 slots): Bestow Curse, Water Walk

4th level (3 slots): **Ice Storm**, Guardian of Faith

5th level (2 slots): Raise Dead, Wall of Stone

ACTIONS

Mace. Melee Weapon Attack: +5 to hit, reach 5 ft., one creature. Hit: 4 (1d6 + 1) bludgeoning damage.

Halberd. Melee Weapon Attack: +5 to hit, reach 10 ft., one creature. Hit: 6 (1d10 + 1) slashing damage.

RESOLUTION

If any of the group are foolish enough to attack them, the priests will beat that person to unconsciousness and then cast Spare The Dying on them so that they won't die.

After the encounter, the priests of Telchur hurry off again on their vital pilgrimage.

Thralls of the Rotting Tree

SUMMARY: The rotting stump of a deceased and corrupted treant has been leeching necrotic energy into the surrounding soil. An insidious fairy ring has sprouted around it and turns hapless travelers into permanent residents.

CR1 225 xp
3 Spore Thralls

CR2 375 xp
5 Spore Thralls

CR3 615 xp
7 Spore Thralls

CR4 875 xp
10 Spore Thralls

CR5 1400 xp
14 Spore Thralls

READ TO THE PLAYERS

Making your way through a swampy region, you notice a circle of mushrooms sprouting from a soggy patch of turf. White statues are scattered around the ring amongst the mushrooms. The statues are shaped like people, but they are composed entirely of white fungi. All the figures are facing the rotting tree stump seen at the center of this thirty foot diameter ring.

COMBAT

Pre-Initiative: The statues are Spore Thralls. The thralls will become active and attack if any of the follow occurs:

- Someone enters the fairy ring.
- Someone approaches within 5 feet of a thrall.
- A thrall is destroyed.

Combat Rounds: Once activated, the thralls will each attack the nearest living person with the goal of killing them. Thralls will continue to attack a fallen PC until dead. A deceased PC's body will be dragged into the circle to decompose. It takes only a few weeks for the corpse to turn into a spore thrall.

If reduced to 0 hitpoints or lured more than 30 feet from the edge of the ring, a thrall will burst, releasing a spore cloud (see sidebar for description).

SPORE THRALL CR 1/4 (50xp)
Medium aberration, neutral evil

Armor Class 8
Hit Points 19 (3d8+6) Speed 20 ft.

STR	DEX	CON	INT	WIS	CHA
13 (+1)	6 (-2)	14 (+2)	3 (-4)	6 (-2)	5 (-3)

Damage Immunities poison
Senses Darkvision 60 Ft., passive Perception 8
Languages –

Spore Cloud. When the thrall is reduced to 0 hit points or moves more than 30 feet from the ring's edge it bursts into a cloud of spores with a 15 foot radius. The cloud then grows. (see sidebar for description)

ACTIONS

Slam. Melee Weapon Attack: +3 to hit, reach 5 ft., one creature. *Hit*: 4 (1d6 + 1) bludgeoning damage.

TREASURE & RESOLUTION

Some minor treasures may be hidden within the exploded husks of each thrall; 1d10 silver coins, 1d6 gold coins, a silver ring, a gold ring, two daggers, a belt buckle, a necklace.

The tree stump in the center of the ring contains within it the dark heart of a corrupted treant. INT(investigation) or WIS(survival) DC 12 to discover the heart. It is a melon-sized mass of heavy, dark wood. An INT(arcana) check of 15 will reveal that this rare heart can be used to close a portal to the Feywild. If the heart passes through a crossing to the Feywild, both the heart and the crossing are destroyed.

SPORE CLOUD

Each Spore Thrall has the potential to burst into a thick cloud of fungal yellow spores with a fifteen foot radius. If they reach 0 hit points or are lured more than 30 feet from the edge of the fairy ring, they pop and leave behind one of these clouds. The cloud's radius grows by another 5 feet with each round. After a minute (ten rounds) the cloud dissipates completely. Clouds can be dispersed by gusts of wind or explosions such as a fireball.

A creature who spends any part of their turn in the cloud will inhale the spores unless they hold their breath for the entirety of that round. Each round that a character inhales spores they suffer 2 points of necrotic damage. A creature can hold its breath continuously for a number of minutes equal to 1 + its Constitution modifier (minimum of 30 seconds).

The spore cloud impairs vision, limiting visibility to 15 feet.

WAGER AGAINST THE WINNER

SUMMARY: A trio of ogres are drinking from a stream when a group of delicious travelers interrupt them. The biggest ogre takes on the party by himself while the other two bet on who will win.

CR1 250 xp
3 Ogrelings

CR2 375 xp
2 Ogrelings
1 Mere Ogre

CR3 500 xp
3 Mere Ogres

CR4 1000 xp
2 Ogrelings
1 Fierce Ogre

CR5 1125 xp
2 Mere Ogres
1 Fierce Ogre

READ TO THE PLAYERS

You come upon a stream. Three putrid ogres who were drinking from the other bank of the stream quickly size you up.
"Tah-tug fight. Beat all!" shouts the biggest of the three ogres as he grabs his greatclub and stomps across the stream.
"Tah-tug no win!" laughs one of the other two.
"Omak say Tag-tug win," replies the other.
"Omak say win, Khleg say no win! Loser no eat! Winner eat double."
"Deal!"
The two ogres on the far side of the stream, Omak and Khleg have chosen their sides in the fight. Neither have greatclubs but they are picking up fist-sized stones from the bank.

COMBAT

Tah-tug is confident that he can smash the party to bits with his greatclub.
Khleg is betting that Tah-tug will lose and hasn't thought out the consequences of that. So, each round he throws a rock at Tah-tug, hoping to sway the battle in favor of the party.
Omak is betting on Tah-tug being victorious. Each round Omak throws a rock at a party member, preferably one not in melee.

If Tah-tug is defeated the other ogres will stop throwing rocks. They simply laugh, and walk away. As they are leaving, if they are attacked or bothered in any way, they will retaliate violently.

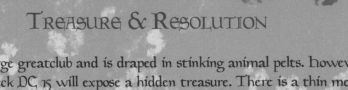

Treasure & Resolution

Tah-Tug only has a large greatclub and is draped in stinking animal pelts. however, an INT(investigation) check DC 15 will expose a hidden treasure. There is a thin metal wand trapped under a flabby fold of skin on the ogre's chest. The food particles lodged in there indicate that it was trapped there by accident while eating the wand's previous owner. The wand is a Wand of the War Mage +1.

Omek and Khleg each have a bag containing 1d6 sp, 2d6 gp, moldy cheese, empty bottles made of colored glass, assorted skulls of animals and people, and 1d4 helmets of varying sizes and designs.

MERE OGRE CR 1 (100xp)
Large giant, chaotic evil

Armor Class 11 (hide armor)
Hit Points 39 (6d8+12)   Speed 40 ft.

STR	DEX	CON	INT	WIS	CHA
18 (+4)	9 (-1)	15 (+2)	5 (-3)	7 (-2)	7 (-2)

Senses Darkvision 60 Ft., passive Perception 8
Languages Common, Giant

ACTIONS
Greatclub. Melee Weapon: +6 to hit, reach 5 ft., one target. *Hit*: 13 (2d8 + 4) bludgeoning damage.

Thrown Rock. Ranged Weapon Attack: +2 to hit, range 30/60 ft., one target. *Hit*: 5 (1d4 + 4) bludgeoning damage.

OGRELING CR 1/2 (50xp)
Large giant, chaotic evil

Armor Class 12 (hide armor)
Hit Points 32 (5d8+10)   Speed 40 ft.

STR	DEX	CON	INT	WIS	CHA
17 (+3)	11 (+0)	15 (+2)	5 (-3)	6 (-2)	6 (-2)

Senses Darkvision 60 Ft., passive Perception 8
Languages Common, Giant

ACTIONS
Slam. Natural Weapon Attack: +5 to hit, reach 5 ft., one target. *Hit*: 6 (1d6 + 3) bludgeoning damage.

Thrown Rock. Ranged Weapon Attack: +2 to hit, range 30/60 ft., one target. *Hit*: 5 (1d4 + 3) bludgeoning damage.

FIERCE OGRE CR 3 (450xp)
Large giant, chaotic evil

Armor Class 11 (hide armor)
Hit Points 67 (9d8+27)   Speed 40 ft.

STR	DEX	CON	INT	WIS	CHA
20 (+5)	8 (-1)	16 (+3)	6 (-2)	7 (-2)	8 (-1)

Senses Darkvision 60 Ft., passive Perception 8
Languages Common, Giant

ACTIONS
Greatclub. Melee Weapon: +7 to hit, reach 5 ft., one target. *Hit*: 14 (2d8 + 5) bludgeoning damage.

ARRIVING ON THE STINKY SIDE

SUMMARY: The party arrives at a walled city at the exact moment of an orc raid.

CR1 250 xp
2 Orcs

CR2 450 xp
3 Orcs

CR3 600 xp
4 Orcs

CR4 900 xp
6 Orcs

CR5 1750 xp
10 Orcs

READ TO THE PLAYERS

As the sun sets, your approach to the high-walled city takes you past the foulest of areas. Not only does the city's sewage drain here but it also appears to be the city's dump, where a dozen filthy dogs root through the garbage for rats and discarded chicken bones.

In sharp contrast, from within the walls comes the sounds of wedding music. A loud, festive marital celebration is clearly happening just beyond.

Perhaps it is the music that draws your attention upward, but you realize that some orcs are launching a raid! The orcs are slowly scaling the high stone wall, intent on murder and pillage.

The nearest city gate is too far to call out to. These orcs will have completed their raid and escaped before help can arrive. One of them is already scaling the wall while the others wait their turn amongst the trash and excrement. A fifty-foot slope of revolting waste stands between you and the base of the wall where many of the orcs have full cover thanks to piles of trash. This is difficult terrain which will halve your speed.

COMBAT

Pre-Initiative: The orcs are not expecting an attack from behind. They can be snuck up on (passive perception 10) but with <u>disadvantage</u> due to walking through sewage and trash.

Round 1: Orcs on the ground will use greataxes in melee or throw javelins from cover.
Any orcs on the wall will attempt to make it to the top. The wall is 40 feet high and the orcs can climb ten feet per round. If they take damage they must make a STR(athletics) check <u>DC equal to the damage</u>, or fall and suffer 1d6 damage per 10 feet. If any orcs make it to the top of the wall they throw javelins down at the PCs.

Round 2: Feeling trapped, the orcs will fight to the death. If not in melee, any orcs on the ground will use their racial bonus action to close the distance to the nearest PC. Some of the dogs begin barking at the combatants.

Round 3: Some of the dogs get so overexcited that they begin biting anyone in melee. Each melee combatant is attacked by one dog. A WIS(animal handling) check DC 14 can convince a dog to stop biting. They will also stop if they take 4 or more damage from any single attack.

Round 4: One of the orcs reveals that he is a priest of the orc god, Gruumsh, by casting his one, and only, healing spell on a fallen or wounded comrade, restoring 9 hitpoints.

Round 5: Any surviving orcs try to flee. Even if winning, the noise of combat has foiled any chance they had at launching a surprise raid.

Treasure & Resolution

The orcs each have a greataxe, three javelins, and a foul, pest-ridden suit of hide armor, each stinking of sewage.

The party members will reek most foully, which would normally prevent them from gaining access to the city. A ChA(persuasion) check DC 12 will convince the gate sentries that they are sincere in having just prevented an orc raid. In that case, the sentries will bring them buckets of water to dump upon themselves and then allow them to pass.

One of the sentries will accompany the PCs to the wedding celebration and explain what happened to the patriarch, Quinbob The Elder. Still smelly, Quinbob does not invite them to the festivities but does offer them free room and board at his inn, The Captain's Poet.

ORC CR 1/2 (100xp)
Medium humanoid (orc), chaotic evil

Armor Class 13 (Hide Armor)
Hit Points 15 (2d8+6) **Speed** 30 ft.

STR	DEX	CON	INT	WIS	CHA
16 (+3)	12 (+1)	16 (+3)	7 (-2)	11 (+0)	10 (+0)

Senses Darkvision 60 ft., passive Perception 10
Languages Common, Orc

Aggressive. As a bonus action, the orc can move up to its speed toward a hostile creature that it can see.

ACTIONS
Greataxe. Melee Weapon Attack: +5 to hit, reach 5 ft., one creature. Hit: 9 (1d12 + 3) slashing damage.

Javelin. Melee or Ranged Weapon Attack: +5 to hit, reach 5 ft. or range 30/120 ft., one target. Hit: 6 (1d6 + 3) piercing damage

DOG CR 1/4 (100xp)
Medium beast, unaligned

Armor Class 12
Hit Points 9 (2d8+0) **Speed** 40 ft.

STR	DEX	CON	INT	WIS	CHA
12 (+1)	15 (+2)	10 (+0)	3 (-4)	8 (-1)	6 (-2)

Skills Perception +3, Stealth +4
Senses passive Perception 13
Languages –

Perceptive. The dog has advantage on perception checks that involve hearing or smell.

ACTIONS
Bite. Melee Weapon Attack: +4 to hit, reach 5 ft., one creature. Hit: 7 (2d4+2) piercing damage.

TEMPEST VS THE WHISKEY DOG

SUMMARY: While staying at The Whiskey Dog Inn & Tavern, a fierce storm strikes. A tornado tears apart the inn piece by piece, putting the party and the other guests in grave danger.

READ TO THE PLAYERS

Your rooms are on the third floor of the inn, away from the tavern revelers on the ground level. You get to enjoy a well-deserved sleep on a mattress packed with fresh straw and pillows stuffed with feathers. But before your long rest is complete, you are awoken by the loudest noise you've ever heard. An unceasing, roaring howl gets louder by the second.

You hear someone yell, "Tornado! Get to the kitchen cellar!"

The roar increases to a deafening volume and is joined by the sounds of splintering wood. Before your eyes the roof and walls begin tearing away into the swirling darkness.

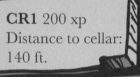

CR1 200 xp
Distance to cellar:
140 ft.

CR2 300 xp
Distance to cellar:
155 ft.

CR3 500 xp
Distance to cellar:
180 ft.

CR4 800 xp
Distance to cellar:
210 ft.

CR5 1200 xp
Distance to cellar:
240 ft.

ACTION

Round by round the characters must each make their way to the kitchen cellar, the only safe place. The distance to the cellar is set by the CR of the encounter. Have the players keep track of their total distance.

Each round players can attempt to move closer to the cellar which means moving to the staircase, down two flights, and across the ground floor to the kitchen. If they drop to 0 hit points they get sucked into the tornado (same as if they had rolled a 1 on the Chaotic Circumstance table).

A Strength(athletics) check determines if they can fight through the wind and debris to move each round. No <u>dash</u> actions are possible.
DC 15: Move at normal speed
DC 10: Move at half speed

Once in the cellar, they can safely wait out the storm with the handful of other people who made it in time.

Raging Chaos

The tornado causes unpredictable events each round. Have each player roll a d20 at the start of each turn to determine what circumstance they face.

D20 Chaotic Circumstance

20 Wind propels them 15 feet closer to their objective.

18-19 A tree branch speeds at them. Dex save DC 10 or take d4 piercing damage.

16-17 A board flies at them. Dex save DC 10 or take d6 bludgeoning damage.

14-15 A chair sails at them. Dex save DC 10 or take 2d4 bludgeoning damage.

12-13 A table races at them. Dex save DC 10 or take 2d6 bludgeoning damage.

10-11 The floor gives way. They drop one level and take 1d6 falling damage but gain 60 feet of advancement towards the goal of reaching the kitchen cellar.

8-9 The wind hurls another guest at them. Dex save DC 10 or 1d8 bludgeoning damage.

7 A cow crashes into them. Dex save DC 10 or take 2d8 bludgeoning damage.

4-6 Big gust of wind. Str save DC 10 or be blown backwards 15 ft.

2-3 Strong gust of wind. Str save DC 12 or be blown backwards 30 ft.

1 Tornado tries pulling them out of the building. Str save DC 12 or be ripped up into the tornado, flung half a mile away, and suffer 1d20 damage.

Treasure & Resolution

When the storm has passed, the inn is demolished. Any possessions the PCs didn't have with them can be found among the inn's wreckage with a INT (investigation) check DC 12. Allow one check per hour of searching to recover their belongings.

A dozen other guests have died in the tornado and some of their belongings will be found among the debris such as shoes, coats, hats, gloves, and coin pouches.

Mounts will be spooked and may have run off if the DM desires the party to proceed on foot.

Tarred and Fettered

Summary: Naturally occurring tar pits and wild magic have mingled in a terrifying new hazard for creatures passing through.

CR1 200 xp
1 Tar Bear

CR2 500 xp
2 Tar Bears

CR3 900 xp
3 Tar Bears

CR4 1200 xp
4 Tar Bears

CR5 1800 xp
6 Tar Bears

Read to the players

You are carefully winding your way around a network of bubbling tar pits. A fog of stinking gases shrouds your view. Visibility is limited to 30 feet. Countless creatures have undoubtedly met their scalding, sticky fate here thanks to a single misstep. Shimmering swirls of color in the tar suggest that wild magic has had an influence here. This notion is confirmed when the top half of a bear explodes from the nearest pit, trailing ropes of sinewy tar.

Arcana Check DC 12:
You think this monstrosity will take extra damage from cold attacks.

Cutting The Fetter

A clever player might attempt to cut the rope-like tether connecting each bear to its pit. It can only be cut by 10 points of slashing damage delivered in a single blow. It instantly heals up any damage less than that. The damage does not affect the bear's hit points. Once severed, the bear howls horrifically and then slumps and dies.

Tar Pit Hazards

The smooth stone footpaths between the pits are narrow and treacherous.
Any movement, beyond a 5ft step, may result in slipping into a bubbling cauldron of tar. During combat, when there is stress and distraction, any movement further than 5ft requires a DEX(acrobatics) check DC 10 to not fall into a pit. Failure means the character has slipped into a pit and their turn is ended.

A character who begins their turn in a pit suffers 1d4 fire damage. To scramble out of a pit a character needs to spend their action to attempt a DC 17 STR(athletics) check. They can make this check with advantage if another character is assisting them.

COMBAT

Round 1 (surprise round):
Roll Initiative. Characters who succeed at a WIS(perception) check of 15 are not surprised and can act this round. The Tar Bear mentioned in the scene description is hurtling through the air, targeting a random PC with its Lunging Slam attack this round.

Round 2: The first Tar Bear is pulled 10 feet per round back into the pit by its tether. If isn't grappling its initial target, it may make a Claw attacks within 5ft. A second tar bear (if CR 2 or higher) launches a Lunging Slam attack from a different tar pit at another random PC.

Round 3+: Each subsequent round, another Tar Bear will make its first attack, each from a different nearby tar pit, until their are no more remaining according to the CR. Once a Tar Bear is reeled back into its pit, it will once again launch at a random PC.

Round 4: One of the pits that a tar bear came from belches out a huge, noxious cloud of yellow vapors. Within a round, these vapors spread over the area of the combat and obscure vision to only 5 feet. At the start of each round, PCs must make a Constitution saving throw DC 10 or be poisoned until the start of their next turn. The yellow vapors dissipate after 4 rounds.

TAR BEAR CR 1 (100xp)
Medium monstrosity, neutral evil

Armor Class 8
Hit Points 19 (3d8+6)   Speed 5 ft.

STR	DEX	CON	INT	WIS	CHA
16 (+3)	6 (-2)	16 (+3)	3 (-4)	3 (-4)	2 (-4)

Skills Athletics +7
Damage Resistances fire, poison
Damage Vulnerabilities cold
Senses Tremorsense 60 Ft., passive Perception 14
Languages –

Tar fetter. After leaping from a pool of tar, the tar powerfully reels the beast back into the pool at a rate of 10 feet per round.

ACTIONS

Lunging Slam. Melee Weapon Attack: +3 to hit, reach 5 ft., one creature. *Hit*: 6 (1d6 + 3) bludgeoning damage and 1d4 fire damage from the intense heat. On a hit, target becomes grappled.

Claw. Melee Weapon Attack: +5 to hit, reach 5 ft., one creature. *Hit*: 6 (1d6 + 3) slashing damage.

TREASURE & RESOLUTION

The bubbling tar pits go quiet and a light breeze sweeps across the land, clearing away the fog. A sense of peace falls over the area.

INT(investigation) DC 12 will uncover a small green crystal stuck to a defeated tar bear or to a part of a tar bear that was severed during the fight.

IOUN STONE OF LIFE FOCUS (UNCOMMON): An emerald green crystal that enhances healing magic. Your healing spells restore 1 extra hitpoint per die rolled.
See page 176 of the DMG for more details about Ioun stones. Requires attunement.

SWORD OF THE SLAIN

SUMMARY: Villagers are gathered to bury a murdered friend. When the party comes past, the mourners jump to dark conclusions about these strangers.

READ TO THE PLAYERS

Entering a picturesque village, you pass by a graveyard, adjacent to the road. A solemn funeral is taking place, attended by a large crowd. A voice from the crowd shouts, "Hey! That's Giffram's sword!"

Then another shouts, "Yeah it is! Those must be the people that killed Giff!"

The crowd of mourners quickly swarms you. You are half encircled. The grief-stricken villagers are enraged, but clearly also nervous about how to exact their fury upon such a heavily armed group of strangers.

CR1 225 xp
6 Villagers

CR2 385 xp
9 Villagers

CR3 600 xp
12 Villagers

CR4 1050 xp
1 Priestess
6 Villagers

CR5 1550 xp
1 Priestess
13 Villagers

DO YOU EXPLAIN THAT THEY ARE MISTAKEN?

Roll CHA(PERSUASION) DC12

OR

DO YOU INTIMIDATE THEM INTO BACKING OFF?

Roll CHA(INTIMIDATION) DC12

You convince them that you don't have Giffram's sword. That doesn't clear you of his murder, though. They recount the circumstances of Giffram's body being found naked by the fishing pond.

ROLL INT(INVESTIGATION) DC12

The villagers don't trust you and persist in hurling accusations. They are building up their courage to attack.

ROLL INT(HISTORY) DC12

They mention Giffram was found naked, including his hobnail boots. You notice that one of the villagers' foot prints in the dirt has a hobnail pattern and accuse him of the crime.

ROLL CHA(PERFORMANCE) DC12

You remind the mob of the laws of the land, demanding that they give you a trial. They decide to hold a trial right then and there in the center of the road.

ROLL CHA(PERFORMANCE) DC12

RESOLUTION 2

The PCs successfully defend themselves and the mob loses its fervor. Though they will feel very unwelcome here now.

RESOLUTION 1

The PCs successfully interrogate, Jotan, the accused man, in the middle of the street, and cause him to confess. Later, overcome with a mix of gratitude and guilt, the village throw the PCs a feast. They give them Giffram's old boots which are more special than anyone knew. These are Boot Of Slow Falling which allow the wearer to halve any damage they suffer from falling. (uncommon, requires attunement.)

VILLAGER CR 1/8 (25xp)

Medium humanoid (human), chaotic good

Armor Class 11
Hit Points 9 (2d6+2) **Speed** 30 ft.

STR	DEX	CON	INT	WIS	CHA
12 (+1)	12 (+1)	12 (+1)	10 (+0)	10 (+0)	10 (+0)

Skills Athletics +3
Senses passive Perception 10
Languages Common

ACTIONS

Simple Weapon Attacks. (dagger, sickle, pitchfork, farming implement) +3 to hit, reach 5 ft., one target. 1d4+1 piercing damage.

VILLAGE PRIESTESS CR 2 (450xp)

Medium humanoid (human), chaotic good

Armor Class 9
Hit Points 40 (6d8+6) **Speed** 30 ft.

STR	DEX	CON	INT	WIS	CHA
10 (+0)	9 (-1)	12 (+1)	10 (+0)	16 (+3)	10 (+0)

Skills Religion +3, Medicine +5
Senses passive Perception 13
Languages Common, Dwarven, Elven

Spellcasting. The priestess is a 6th-level cleric. Her spellcasting ability is Wisdom (spell save DC 15, to hit with spell attacks +5). Her preferred combat spells are **bolded**.

Cantrips (at will): Light, Resistance, Guidance, **Spare the Dying**

1st level (4 slots): Bless, Cure Wounds, **Healing Word**, Purify Food & Drink

2nd level (3 slots): Calm Emotions, Lesser Restoration, **Hold Person**

3rd level (3 slots): Remove Curse, **Spirit Guardians**, Tongues

ACTIONS

Quarterstaff. +3 to hit, reach 5 ft., one target. 1d6-1 bludgeoning damage.

THE VILLAGERS ATTACK!

Roll Initiative. Only the menfolk of fighting age will attack. The women, children, and elderly simply cheer or cry, and they stay clear of the melee.

Round 1: The villagers attack with fury.

Round 2: The villagers continue their melee attacks. If they can manage to fell a PC, they will take his/her weapons and use them.

Round 3+: Attacks continue until the PCs outnumber the villagers, at which point the villagers lose their mob mentality and retreat.

RESOLUTION 3

If the party is victorious, the remaining villagers beg for mercy and attend to their wounded. If the PCs are beaten, they will awake to find themselves bound to fence posts with rope and awaiting the arrival of the local legal authority.

BALEFUL BREAKOUT

SUMMARY: Cultists of the god of regret have been imprisoned and awaiting execution for the crime of sowing discord. They have weakened the walls of their prison and are about to escape.

CR1 250 xp
2 Cultists

CR2 450 xp
3 Cultists

CR3 600 xp
4 Cultists

CR4 900 xp
6 Cultists

CR5 1750 xp
10 Cultists

READ TO THE PLAYERS

Walking down the cobblestone streets of the city, a sprinkle of masonry flakes fall upon your faces. You are passing by a three story prison tower at the moment and look up just in time to see part of the wall, 15 feet up, suddenly push out, raining large stones down upon your heads!

Call for Dexterity saving throws DC 13 to avoid the falling masonry stones. Failure means suffering 1d6 damage per the CR of the encounter (i.e. CR2=2d6, CR3=3d6)

From the hole in the wall above you now, a shabbily-dressed woman with matted hair climbs out and drops to the ground. She is quickly followed by another woman of similar appearance. A uniformed soldier leans out of a window on the third floor. He shouts at you, "Stop those prisoners!" The women aren't waiting to find out how civic-minded you are. They attack you with the long, black, sinister-looking nails of their left hands, still powdered with masonry dust.

COMBAT BEGINS Roll Initiative.

Round 1: The two prisoners, who already exited the hole, attack the party. Any additional combatants, listed in the CR, exit through the hole this round and drop to the ground. They will be ready to attack on round 2. From above, the prison guard shouts, "Keep them there! We're coming down!"

Round 2: One of the women begins hissing an unearthly, terrifying chant. The others quickly join in, continuing their vicious claw swipes while they chant. Damage to the women does not interrupt their chant. Only a silence spell can stop them.

Round 3: The magic of the chant takes hold. Each time a player wants to make a melee attack against a cultist, they must first make a Wisdom saving throw DC 13. Failure means they are unnerved by fear and the attack is made with disadvantage.

Rounds 4+: The heavy door to the tower slams open and guards pour out. Any surviving cultists will disengage and flee into the city. The guards pursue them. One older guard stops to thank the party for their help.

CULTIST CR 1/2 (100xp)
Medium humanoid, chaotic evil

Armor Class 11
Hit Points 22 (5d8) **Speed** 30 ft.

STR	DEX	CON	INT	WIS	CHA
12(+1)	12(+1)	11(+0)	10(+0)	11(+0)	15(+2)

Senses passive Perception 10
Languages Common, Abyssal

Iron Nails. Cultists have the spell-like ability to grow the finger nails of their left hand by four inches.

ACTIONS

Claw. Melee Weapon Attack: +3 to hit, reach 5 ft., one creature. Hit: 6 (2d4+1) slashing damage.

TREASURE & RESOLUTION

The guard will ask the party's help in stabilizing any fallen cultists and bringing them back into the tower, to be placed in a more secure cell. If they help him, allow them each an INT (investigation) check DC 12 (or passive check) to notice there is something hidden in the matted hair of one of them. It is a tiny curved flute carved from a rib bone.

Flute of Foul Utterance (uncommon, requires attunement) When played, this flute makes no noticeable sound except to one target creature within 60 feet. Failing a Charisma save of 13 results in the target blurting out their most shameful and regrettable thoughts and memories for as long as they hear the flute's song. The victim can trace the source of the song as they would any sound.

MOON WILLOW MARIONETTE

SUMMARY: The party makes camp beneath a magical tree that manifests a childhood nightmare.

CR1 - CR5 450 xp
1 Marionette

READ TO ONE CHOSEN PLAYER

You are dreaming, having a nightmare about a childhood bully who terrified you when you were young. The bully has you pinned to the ground, his hands around your neck, slowly choking you to death. Shocked awake, you find yourself still staring into the face of your bully. He is real and hovering above you, suspended by the branches of the willow tree you camped beneath, like a life-size marionette. Your air is cut off by his grasping wooden hands. You can't breathe! You can't call out for help!

COMBAT

Pre-initiative: If any characters are on watch they should automatically notice the assault taking place. Allow other sleeping characters to wake up and join in as soon as there is enough noise to rouse them.

Round 1: The victim being choked is considered grappled. They can get out of the grapple using DEX(acrobatics) or STR(athletics) vs the marionette's athletics check. Choking inflicts 5 points of damage each round. Once the marionette takes any hit point damage, he stops choking his victim and switches to punching attacks.

Round 2: The intense concentration needed for spellcasting draws the marionette towards anyone who casts a spell. He will attack at the nearest PC who cast a spell on their turn. If no targets have cast a spell, he will punch at his original victim.

Rounds 3 thru 5: The marionette continues attacking at whomever casts a spell or whomever is closest. It will not attack anyone who is unconscious.

Rounds 6+: The manifestation begins fading. The marionette loses 1d10 hitpoints per round as it loses its shape.

Useful Skill Checks

INT(nature) DC 12: This is an extremely rare moon willow tree. It is said to have roots which extend into the ethereal plane and is vulnerable to Force damage.

INT(history) DC 12: An old bard's tale recalls how one hero's dream was manifested by a tree. It was his true love. She existed only for a minute and then turned back into a tree branch.

MARIONETTE CR 2 (450xp)

Medium plant, unaligned

Armor Class 16 (natural armor)
Hit Points 95 (10d12+30) **Speed** 40 ft.

STR	DEX	CON	INT	WIS	CHA
18 (+4)	16 (+3)	16 (+3)	2 (-4)	2 (-4)	2 (-4)

Skills Athletics +4
Damage Resistances bludgeoning, piercing
Damage Vulnerabilities force, fire
Senses passive Perception 6
Languages –

Tethered. The marionette cannot move more than 90 feet from its original position.

ACTIONS

Punch. Melee Weapon Attack: +6 to hit, reach 5 ft., one target. 6 (1d4+4) bludgeoning damage.

TREASURE & RESOLUTION

A pale blue ichor is dripping from the remaining husk of the manifestation. An INT(arcana) check DC 15 reveals that this ichor can be used to animate objects. If collected in a wine skin or water skin, there is enough ichor to animate 2d4+2 objects as if by the Animate Objects spell. The ichor must be poured over the object to be animated, a process that takes a full minute.

The moon willow is exhausted and won't manifest another dream for at least 10 years.

DRAINING A HORRID HIDEAWAY

SUMMARY: The drainage exit from a harpy lair catches the party's attention and may lead one of them into a deadly situation.

READ TO THE PLAYERS

The sound of trickling water draws your attention to the base of the cliff. From a fissure in the rock, water steadily drips onto a pile of rancid debris that must have exited from the same place. Among the small pile you see various bones, feathers, fur, and a glint of gold.

CR1 500 xp
2 Harpies

CR2 500 xp
2 Harpies

CR3 900 xp
3 Harpies

CR4 1200 xp.
4 Harpies

CR5 1800 xp
6 Harpies

INFORMATION & SKILL CHECKS

There are 3 gold coins and 6 silver ones in the small pile of refuse. The scraps of fur represent whatever medium-sized grazing animals live in the area. There is a variety of feathers but an INT(nature) or WIS(survival) check DC 12 reveals that the largest of the feathers are not from any known bird. A DC 18 alerts them that the big ones were shed from a harpy.

The drainage hole and the entire chute is very narrow. Only a small-sized character or a skinny medium-sized character (one with a strength under 10) can hope to fit inside. Even still, they will need to make DEX(acrobatics) checks DC 10 every 50 feet along the 200 foot passage, contorting their body to squeeze past tight turns. A critical failure on any of these checks means the character gets stuck until they can eventually hit a DC 20. Subsequent critical failures result in a level in exhaustion.

The harpy cave is high above and on the opposite side of the cliff/mountain. It is inaccessible except by a difficult climb and also concealed by vegetation.

The player must roll DEX(stealth) against the harpies' passive perception (10). If they get caught and need to retreat back down the hole in a hurry, they must make an Acrobatics check DC 10. Otherwise they aren't fully inside and the harpies will attempt to grapple them and pull them out. One of them may also attempt to use Luring Song to draw them back out.

HARPY CR 1 (200xp)
Medium monstrosity, chaotic evil

Armor Class 11
Hit Points 38 (7d8+7) Speed 20 ft., fly 40 ft.

STR	DEX	CON	INT	WIS	CHA
12 (+1)	13 (+1)	12(+0)	7 (-2)	10 (+0)	13 (+1)

Skills Perception +4, Stealth +5
Senses passive Perception 10
Languages Common

ACTIONS

Multiattack. The harpy makes two attacks: one with its claws and one with its club.

Claws. Melee weapon attack: +3 to hit, reach 5 ft., one target. Hit: 6 (2d4 + 1) slashing damage.

Club. Melee weapon attack: +3 to hit, reach 5 ft., one target. Hit: 3 (1d4 + 1) bludgeoning damage.

Luring song. The harpy sings a magical melody. Every humanoid hearing the song must succeed on a DC 11 Wisdom saving throw or be charmed until the song ends. The harpy must take a bonus action on its subsequent turns to continue singing. While charmed, a target is incapacitated and ignores the songs of other harpies. If the charmed target is more than 5 feet away from the harpy, the target must move on its turn toward the harpy by the most direct route, trying to get within 5 feet. A charmed target can repeat the saving throw at the end of each of its turns and as a reaction to taking damage. Creatures that successfully save become immune to this ability.

TREASURE & RESOLUTION

If the harpies notice the intruder, and he gets away, they will fly out of their lair to search for him. They will likely spy his companions and attack them long before the intruder can make it back down the drain.

Each harpy has one special feather on their forehead. These feathers are a foot long and brilliantly colored. They can sell for as much as 5 gold each to a fine clothier. INT(arcana) DC 12 reveals these feathers can also substitute for the normal material component of the hypnotic Pattern spell.

The ornate dagger found in the harpy lair can only be attuned by a character who casts divine spells. It is a +1 dagger which deals double dice damage to fiends.

WEREWOLVES NOT WELCOME

SUMMARY:

Forest gnomes don't want the party traveling through their land for fear they might be werewolves.

READ TO THE PLAYERS

A group of forest gnomes appear in your path and block your passage.

"You canna' go through 'ere," says the bearded leader of the group. "We want no big folks comin' through our valley. You be havin' to go 'round them hills."

You know that circumventing this valley would mean slowing your journey by at least a day.

IF PLAYERS INQUIRE AS TO THE REASON

Roll CHA(PERSUASION) DC12

The gnome replies to you, "Tis our land and no accursed souls are welcome onto it."

ROLL INT(RELIGION) DC12

The gnome replies to you, "We had gone and let big folks in afore and they had the curse of the wolf upon them. Murdered an entire family. We canna take that chance agin!"

ROLL CHA(PERSUASION) DC14

The party deduces they are suspected of being werewolves. They could offer to prove they aren't werewolves by eating wolfsbane leaves. The gnomes will agree to that but the party will first have to go search for some of the poisonous plants.

ROLL WIS(SURVIVAL) DC14

You succeed in convincing the gnomes that you are not werewolves. They are apologetic for having accused you.

ROLL INT(NATURE) DC14

They have acquired the wolfsbane and can bring it back to eat in front of the gnomes.

ROLL Constitution saving throw DC10

On a failed save, the character becomes obviously nauseous. If any of them fail the save, use the resolution below. If all of them save go to the dialog box on the left.

RESOLUTION 1

The character who rolled the nature check notices blue upon the tips of the gnomes' beards and correctly deduce that it is Niddlespurn, the forest gnome holiday celebrating the god of berries. Impressed by their knowledge of their traditions, the gnomes invite the PCs to share in their feast of berry pies and blue ale. They are given a secure place to make camp and valuable information useful to the adventure ahead.

RESOLUTION 2

While the gnomes no longer believe the party has any werewolves, they remain suspicious. They allow the party passage through the valley, though under heavy guard. They are escorted quickly and any locals they pass shrink away in fear.

Wall Of Thorns

6th-level conjuration
Casting Time: 1 action
Range: 120 feet
Components: V, S, M (a handful of thorns)
Duration: Concentration, up to 10 minutes

You create a wall of tough, pliable, tangled brush bristling with needle-sharp thorns. The wall appears within range on a solid surface and lasts for the duration. You choose to make the wall up to 60 feet long, 10 feet high, and 5 feet thick or a circle that has a 20-foot diameter and is up to 20 feet high and 5 feet thick. The wall blocks line of sight.

When the wall appears, each creature within its area must make a Dexterity saving throw. On a failed save, a creature takes 7d8 piercing damage, or half as much damage on a successful save.

A creature can move through the wall, albeit slowly and painfully. For every 1 foot a creature moves through the wall, it must spend 4 feet of movement. Furthermore, the first time a creature enters the wall on a turn or ends its turn there, the creature must make a Dexterity saving throw. It takes 7d8 slashing damage on a failed save, or half as much damage on a successful one.

Forest Gnome Defender

CR 1/2 (100xp)
Small humanoid (gnome), Chaotic Good

Armor Class 13 (Hide Armor)
Hit Points 16 (3d8+3)   **Speed** 30 ft.

STR	DEX	CON	INT	WIS	CHA
12 (+1)	14 (+2)	12 (+1)	12 (+1)	12 (+1)	10 (+0)

Skills Stealth +6
Senses Darkvision 60 ft., passive Perception 11
Languages Common, Gnomish

Home Turf. They can make a Stealth check as a bonus action to hide when in their home valley.

Actions

Light Crossbow. Ranged Weapon Attack: +4 to hit, range 80 ft., Hit: 4 (1d8) piercing damage.

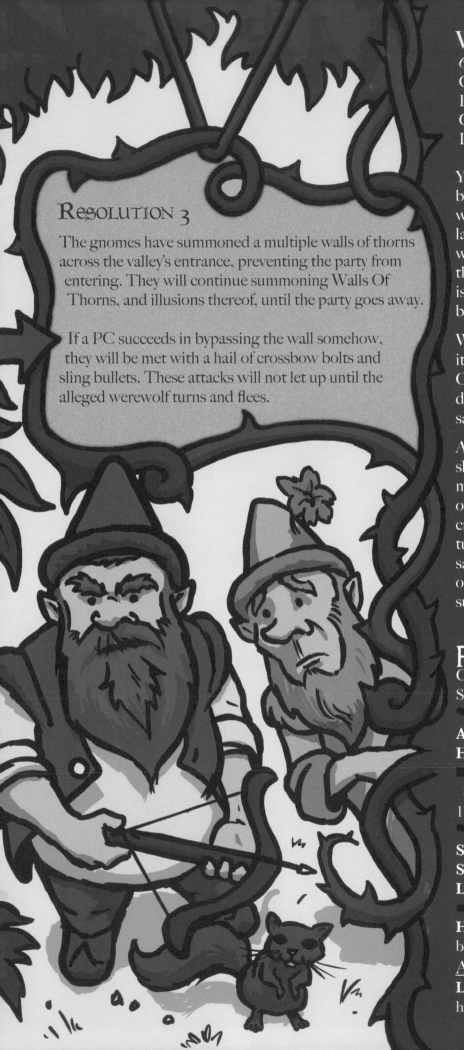

Resolution 3

The gnomes have summoned a multiple walls of thorns across the valley's entrance, preventing the party from entering. They will continue summoning Walls Of Thorns, and illusions thereof, until the party goes away.

If a PC succeeds in bypassing the wall somehow, they will be met with a hail of crossbow bolts and sling bullets. These attacks will not let up until the alleged werewolf turns and flees.

STING OF RIPE BERRIES

SUMMARY: Giant wasps have been feeding upon animals that come to eat from their berry bush.

CR1 250 xp
2 Giant wasps

CR2 450 xp
3 Giant wasps

CR3 600 xp
4 Giant wasps

CR4 900 xp
6 Giant wasps

CR5 1750 xp
10 Giant wasps

READ TO THE PLAYERS

Rounding a tranquil lake, you spy a broken, flipped-over cart, overgrown with vines. Even from twenty feet away you can see the vine is fruiting with plump red berries.

INT(nature) or WIS(survival) or WIS(medicine) check DC 14: Those are owl berries, a very rare species. Even more rare is to find one with ripe berries. They are usually eaten by animals long before they can ripen. It is said that the juice of owl berries can bestow incredible night vision.

COMBAT

Pre-Initiative: The wasps are asleep inside the overturned cart. They are sensitive to vibrations and will be disturbed if anyone comes within 5 feet (unless a DEX(stealth) check of 15 is made). They quickly crawl out of their home and take to the air with a deafening roar of beating wings.

Round 1: Up to three giant wasps emerge to make stinging attacks against the party this round. They will not gang up on a target but will spread their attacks out evenly among all targets within 50 feet.

Round 2: Up to three more giant wasps (see the CR listing)emerge to join the fight.

Round 3: Any remaining wasps enter the fray.

Rounds 4+: Select one character randomly from among all those characters who have been stung, even if they made their saves. This character suddenly discovers they have an allergy to wasp stings. Their throat and eyes begin swelling shut. They are at disadvantage to all checks and attack rolls. Anything that would normally cure a disease or cure a poison will relieve this allergic episode. If untreated, they will become incapacitated after two minutes. The swelling will subside naturally after an hour.

GIANT WASP CR 1/2 (100xp)
Small beast, unaligned

Armor Class 12
Hit Points 13 (3d8) **Speed** 10 ft., fly 50 ft.

STR	DEX	CON	INT	WIS	CHA
10 (+3)	14 (+1)	10 (+3)	1 (-5)	10 (+0)	3 (-4)

Skills Perception +4
Senses passive Perception 14

ACTIONS
Sting. Melee Weapon Attack: +4 to hit, reach 5 ft., one creature.
Hit: 5 (1d6 + 2) piercing damage plus 10 (3d6) poison damage. The target takes only half the poison damage with a DC 11 constitution save. If the poison damage reduces the target to 0 hit points, the target is stable, but paralyzed and poisoned for 1 hour, even after regaining hit points.

Useful Skill Check

WIS(survival) check DC 14: Giant wasps do not like getting wet and they are fearful of getting splashed.
As mentioned in the description, there is a lake very close by. Should a wasp get splashed and fail a DC 14 DEX save, they can no longer fly. They have a swim speed of 0.

TREASURE & RESOLUTION

There are enough ripe owl berries to squeeze out 6 doses of juice. Each dose grants the user 2 hours of darkvision out to 30 feet, or an additional 30 feet of darkvision for those who already have it. Consuming multiple doses doesn't extend the duration or increase the potency.

An investigation of the wasps' nest, beneath the cart, will uncover a collection of small animal skeletons, including an indigo terrapin, whose highly prized iridescent shell is often carved to make jewel-like buttons and jewelry.

It's Raining Wraiths

SUMMARY: A rain storm unveils the spurned spirits of those sacrificed in an ancient ritual.

CR1 225 xp
2 Rain Wraiths

CR2 375 xp
4 Rain Wraiths

CR3 450 xp
6 Rain Wraiths

CR4 875 xp
9 Rain Wraiths

CR5 1850 xp
14 Rain Wraiths

Read to the Players

It is raining while you travel. Not so much that you need to take shelter, but enough that you feel the need to pull your cloaks a little tighter around you. Tiny rivulets stream down the sides of your faces and into your ears. You shake it off, but it persists, forcibly pulsing into your ears. And now your eyes and nose are also under assault! You hear voices in your water-filled ears whispering incomprehensible words. Brushing water from your eyes you see the shapes of people formed of raindrops, their hands grasping for your faces.

Useful Skill Check

INT(religion) check DC 14: By their appearance and mad whispers, you ascertain these people were sacrificed to a god of agriculture or weather in exchange for rain. But the gods withhold their blessings for their own reasons. The offering of these sacrificed souls must have been rejected, leaving their spirits adrift. This means they are undead and susceptible to the magics that affect undead creatures. You believe also that a Destroy Water spell would devastate them.

COMBAT

Rounds 1 thru 4: The Rain Wraiths attempt to press their hands into the faces of the adventurers, causing necrotic damage. Only one wraith can attack a person at a time and so they will spread themselves around appropriately. They are angry, confused, and vengeful.

Round 5: The wraiths pull a bolt of lightning from the storm which strikes a random PC. It does 3d10 lightning damage but only half if a dexterity save succeeds (DC 15).

Round 6+: The wraiths continue their attacks until destroyed.

TREASURE & RESOLUTION

Any non-magical weapon that made a killing strike to a rain wraith now has a faint glow. The destruction of the spirit deposited a spiritual residue on the weapon. This coating allows its wielder to reroll a critically fumbled attack once per day. Requires attunement.

RAIN WRAITH CR 1/4 (50xp)
Medium undead, neutral evil

Armor Class 13
Hit Points 10 (4d8-8) Speed 0 ft., fly 40 ft. (hover)

STR	DEX	CON	INT	WIS	CHA
5 (-3)	16 (+3)	6 (-2)	4 (-3)	4 (-3)	5 (-3)

Damage resistances acid, cold, fire; bludgeoning, piercing, and slashing from nonmagical attacks that aren't silvered
Damage immunities lightning, necrotic, poison, thunder
Condition immunities charmed, exhaustion, grappled, paralyzed, petrified, poisoned, prone, restrained
Senses Blindsight 60 Ft., passive Perception 14
Languages languages known in life

Living Rain. A rain wraith can only manifest on the material plane through falling rain. If the rain stops falling the wraith returns to the ethereal plane. If caught in the area of a Destroy Water spell, the wraith is destroyed utterly without a saving throw.

ACTIONS

Probing grasp. Melee Weapon Attack: +7 to hit, reach 5 ft., one creature. Hit: 8 (2d4 + 3) necrotic damage and Strength save DC 11 or be blinded for 1 round.

Unfamiliar Situation

Summary: A senile old wizard has made life unbearable for his koala bear familiar.

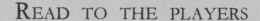

cottage in distance

Read to the Players

A tiny, bear-like creature is desperately trying to show his note to the locals who pass by. They are purposely ignoring him and hurrying on their way. Seeing you, he hobbles over on his stubby legs and desperately waves his note in your direction.

If the players take the note, cover this half of the encounter and show them the adjacent illustration.

Treasure & Resolution

Conrad's cottage is sparse. Janxy has traded nearly all the wizard's possessions over the years for food and firewood. All that remains of value are some jars of wizard's ink, a small traveling spellbook, some kitchen supplies, and that wand that Conrad has relied on.

Janxy simply climbs up into his bed and goes to sleep.

Janxy, the familiar, is being abused by his senile old wizard, Conrad Inkmaker. Running away is not an option and, while he cannot talk, Janxy will happily lead the party to the musty, ivy-covered cottage of his master.

The old wizard spends all his time in a rocking chair by the fireplace muttering to himself. He is delusional and paranoid. Spellcasting is no longer an option for him but he has a wand and uses it all too often. In fact, as soon as the party enters the cottage, Conrad will immediately start zapping them with it. It is the only action he can take.

Wand of Shivers, rare (requires attunement)

This wand has 7 charges. While holding it, you can use an action to expend 1 of its charges to cause a ghostly ray to streak from the tip toward a creature you can see within 60 feet of you. The target suffers 1d6 cold damage and must succeed on a DC 15 Constitution saving throw or be <u>frightened</u> for 1 minute. At the end of each of the target's turns, it can repeat the saving throw, ending the effect on itself on a success. The wand regains 1d6 + 1 expended charges daily at dawn. If you expend the wand's last charge, roll a d20. On a 1, the wand crumbles into ashes and is destroyed.

my master be a
wizard of ill
temper who treat
me most cruel.
Kindly help,
Janxy

UNINVITED BEDFELLOW

SUMMARY: Mischievous pixies play a prank on the party while they sleep.

READ TO A PLAYER KEEPING WATCH OR TO THE FIRST ONE TO WAKE.

You glance around at your sleeping companions. Something strikes you as odd and it takes a moment to realize what exactly has captured your attention. There are one too many people asleep here.

One of your companions is asleep in two different spots. They have an identical twin!

CR1 225 xp
3 Pooks

CR2 375 xp
4 Pooks

CR3 450 xp
6 Pooks

CR4 875 xp
9 Pooks

CR5 1850 xp
14 Pooks

One of the PCs has an exact duplicate. The pooks have all physically combined to form this perfect copy. The copy acts, sounds, and feels exactly like the PC. The only flaw is smell. They cannot copy smell. INT(investigation) DC 18 uncovers the ruse by smell

When the PC speaks, the copy speaks the same words simultaneously. When addressed directly, the copy will assert that it is the original and not the copy.

Using Detect Magic is of little help. The pooks have cast Nystuls Magic Aura (PHB pg 263) upon the PC so that both subjects appear magic.

Eventually the ruse will end, either because the PCs have figured it out or because the pooks have lost interest in the game, and the copy will dissolve into a cloud of 18 pooks. Some pooks simply fly away laughing but the rest, those listed in the CR, attack the player characters.

COMBAT

Round 1: The pooks fly around the camp zapping people randomly with their Shocking Grasp attacks. They may prefer to attack those wearing metal armor since they have advantage on those attacks.

Rounds 2 & 3: They focus their attacks only on PCs who have successfully injured a pook. If no pooks are injured they continue to attack randomly.

Round 4: One pook grabs a small item and flies off with it. This provokes an opportunity attack from a PC. The pook will grab one of the following items: 1d6: 1. boot, 2.mess kit, 3. tinder box, 4. potion, 5. hat or helmet, 6. knife or dagger.

Round 5: Any remaining pooks grab small items in plain sight and fly off with them, provoking opportunity attacks.

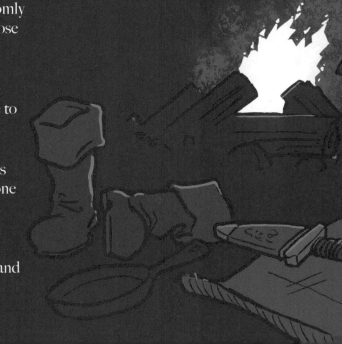

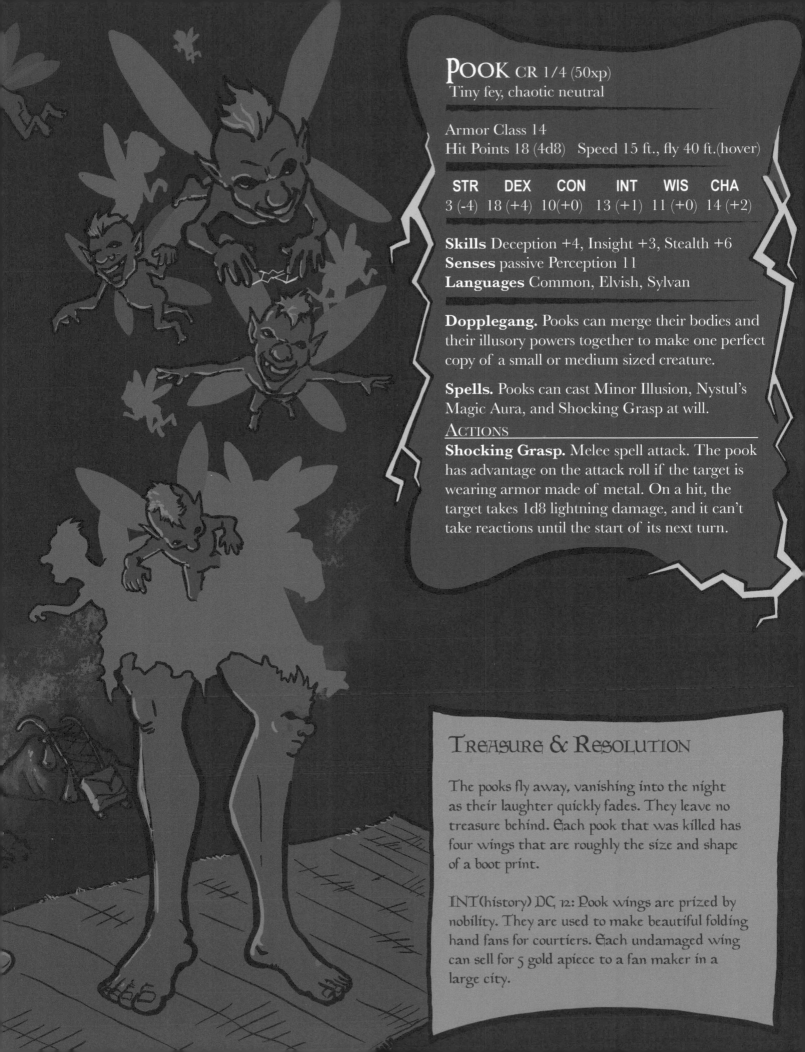

POOK CR 1/4 (50xp)
Tiny fey, chaotic neutral

Armor Class 14
Hit Points 18 (4d8) Speed 15 ft., fly 40 ft.(hover)

STR	DEX	CON	INT	WIS	CHA
3 (-4)	18 (+4)	10(+0)	13 (+1)	11 (+0)	14 (+2)

Skills Deception +4, Insight +3, Stealth +6
Senses passive Perception 11
Languages Common, Elvish, Sylvan

Dopplegang. Pooks can merge their bodies and their illusory powers together to make one perfect copy of a small or medium sized creature.

Spells. Pooks can cast Minor Illusion, Nystul's Magic Aura, and Shocking Grasp at will.

ACTIONS

Shocking Grasp. Melee spell attack. The pook has advantage on the attack roll if the target is wearing armor made of metal. On a hit, the target takes 1d8 lightning damage, and it can't take reactions until the start of its next turn.

TREASURE & RESOLUTION

The pooks fly away, vanishing into the night as their laughter quickly fades. They leave no treasure behind. Each pook that was killed has four wings that are roughly the size and shape of a boot print.

INT(history) DC 12: Pook wings are prized by nobility. They are used to make beautiful folding hand fans for courtiers. Each undamaged wing can sell for 5 gold apiece to a fan maker in a large city.

Betrayal of the Beard

Summary: A parasite pretending to be a character's beard just wants to be ignored.

CR1 200 xp
Life Drain 1d4

CR2 300 xp
Life Drain 1d6

CR3 450 xp
Life Drain 1d8

CR4 650 xp
Life Drain 2d6

CR5 900 xp
Life Drain 3d6

Prelude to the Encounter

The encounter requires at least one of the party members to have a beard and for the party to find succulent fruit such as pears or peaches. These can be plucked from a tree in passing or purchased from a shop or vendor. In either case, you should remark about how juicy they are and how the juice is running down their chins.

The Encounter

The next day one of the bearded PCs wakes to discover their beard has grown dramatically. It is not magic. The extended beard is a parasitic creature called a furlock that attaches to hair or fur and draws nutrients from the host through the follicles. The PC's maximum hitpoints are reduced by 2 while the furlock is attached.

If injured, the furlock randomly attacks at everything around in a five foot radius, including the host itself. The fibers of the creature can stretch and the tips become rigid like pins. The furlock will thrash around wildly like this for as long as it is injured and for 3 rounds afterward. Then it will return to its camouflaged state.

Useful Skill Check

WIS(medicine) check DC 17: The creature is a parasite called a Furlock that grows on fur or hair. After growing to a length of a few feet, clumps of the furlock will periodically drop off. These are eventually used by birds as nesting materials. If landing in a fruit tree, the furlock spores can then infect nearby fruit and continue the cycle.

The prescribed treatment is to cut the host's hairs above where the furlock is attached. Because it is so difficult to distinguish between furlock and hair, it is best to cut the hairs as close the skin as possible.

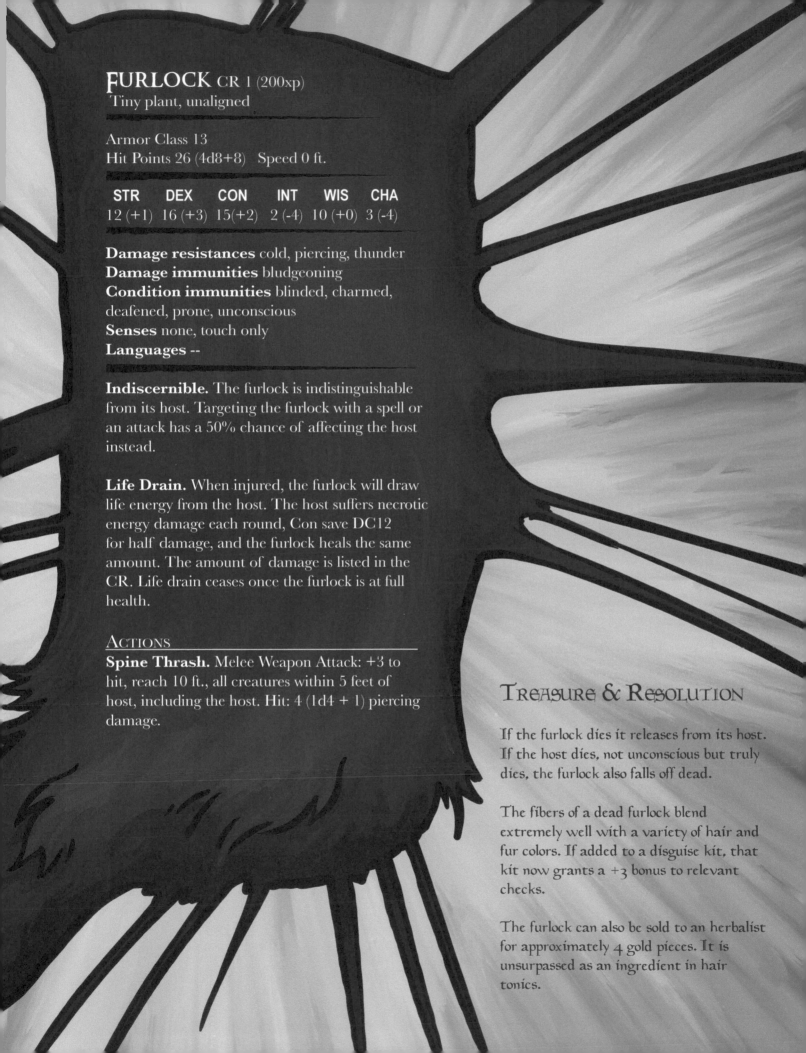

FURLOCK CR 1 (200xp)
Tiny plant, unaligned

Armor Class 13
Hit Points 26 (4d8+8)   Speed 0 ft.

STR	DEX	CON	INT	WIS	CHA
12 (+1)	16 (+3)	15 (+2)	2 (-4)	10 (+0)	3 (-4)

Damage resistances cold, piercing, thunder
Damage immunities bludgeoning
Condition immunities blinded, charmed,
deafened, prone, unconscious
Senses none, touch only
Languages --

Indiscernible. The furlock is indistinguishable
from its host. Targeting the furlock with a spell or
an attack has a 50% chance of affecting the host
instead.

Life Drain. When injured, the furlock will draw
life energy from the host. The host suffers necrotic
energy damage each round, Con save DC12
for half damage, and the furlock heals the same
amount. The amount of damage is listed in the
CR. Life drain ceases once the furlock is at full
health.

ACTIONS
Spine Thrash. Melee Weapon Attack: +3 to
hit, reach 10 ft., all creatures within 5 feet of
host, including the host. Hit: 4 (1d4 + 1) piercing
damage.

TREASURE & RESOLUTION

If the furlock dies it releases from its host.
If the host dies, not unconscious but truly
dies, the furlock also falls off dead.

The fibers of a dead furlock blend
extremely well with a variety of hair and
fur colors. If added to a disguise kit, that
kit now grants a +3 bonus to relevant
checks.

The furlock can also be sold to an herbalist
for approximately 4 gold pieces. It is
unsurpassed as an ingredient in hair
tonics.

DEAD END EXIT

SUMMARY: When the PCs try to leave the city, they are told that gate is closed and directed to the next nearest gate, leading them into an ambush.

READ TO THE PLAYERS

As you head for the nearest city gate, a young guard steps into your path. "Champion's gate is closed, m'lords," says the guard. "If'n yer leavin' the city yer best take Armory street to Minstrel's gate." He points you in the direction of the detour and bids you a good day.

> The players can short circuit this encounter by simply not going down Armory street. Unless they are from this city, they won't know Armory street is a dead end. The guard is an actual city guard using his uniform to direct these travelers into a trap.

Armory street is desolate, populated only by a few beggars and a drunkard urinating against one of the boarded up buildings. Turning the corner you find yourself staring at another high wall. This is a dead end.

Behind you a group of young people grin menacingly as they pull clubs from within the folds of their filthy clothes. The guard that sent you down this street steps up to join in the ambush.

CR1 600 xp
2 Urchins
1 Guardsman

CR2 750 xp
3 Urchins
1 Guardsman

CR3 900 xp
4 Urchins
1 Guardsman

CR4 1050 xp
5 Urchins
1 Guardsman

CR5 1925 xp
9 Urchins
1 Guardsman

AVOIDING COMBAT

Tactic 1: WIS(perception) DC 12: This gang of young people all share a family resemblance. Also, one of them appears to be ill but putting on a brave face. WIS(medicine) DC 15: The sick one has the symptoms of Red Rat Fever, a deadly disease common to malnourished street urchins.

Tactic 2: WIS(insight) DC 14: These kids can probably be intimidated into backing down. CHA(intimidation) DC 14 will cause them to apologize and switch their tactic to begging for money to help their brother. They need 20 gp to pay a healer to Remove Disease.

URCHIN CR 1/2 (100xp)
Medium humanoid, chaotic neutral

Armor Class 12
Hit Points 27 (5d8+5)   **Speed** 30 ft.

STR	DEX	CON	INT	WIS	CHA
12 (+1)	14 (+2)	12 (+1)	11 (+0)	12 (+1)	10 (+0)

Senses Acrobatics +5, Stealth +5
Senses passive Perception 11
Languages Common

Pack Tactics. An urchin has advantage on an attack roll against a creature if at least one of the urchin's allies is within 5 feet of the creature and the ally isn't incapacitated.

ACTIONS
Club. Melee Weapon Attack: +3 to hit, reach 5 ft., one creature. Hit: 3 (1d4 + 1) bludgeoning.

COMBAT

Round 1: The urchins don't want to fight but are desperate. They are bolstered by the presence of their big brother, the city guardsman. They all attack except the sick one who instead casts Vicious Mockery at one of the fighter types, hurling a startling stream of insults at the fighter. (Wisdom save DC 13 or suffer 1d4 psychic damage and disadvantage on next attack.)

Round 2: The sick one casts Vicious Mockery again and his siblings all focus their attacks on that same target.

Round 3: The sick brother once again tries to cast his spell but vomits halfway through and falls to his knees. The others move towards him, attacking whomever is closest to him.

Rounds 4+: The siblings are rattled and have lost their confidence. They will try to retreat if they can do so without leaving anyone behind.

GUARDSMAN CR 1 (200xp)
Medium humanoid, chaotic neutral

Armor Class 14 (Studded Leather)
Hit Points 55 (10d8+10)   **Speed** 30 ft.

STR	DEX	CON	INT	WIS	CHA
15 (+2)	15 (+2)	12 (+1)	12 (+1)	12 (+1)	14 (+2)

Senses passive Perception 11
Languages Common

Pack Tactics. See Urchin above

ACTIONS
Flail. Melee Weapon Attack: +6 to hit, reach 5 ft., one creature. Hit: 6 (1d8 + 2) bludgeoning.

TREASURE & RESOLUTION

These kids have absolutely nothing of value. however, if the party saved the boy from his disease, either by paying for the healer or healing him themselves, the boy gives them his pet rat, Tumbler. Tumbler has been trained to reach his paws into locks and push up the pins. Using Tumbler, you can attempt to open a standard key lock with an Animal handling check instead of a Thieves Tools check.

ELEPHANT ARCHERS

SUMMARY: Goblin marauders have tamed an elephant to serve as a mobile firing platform.

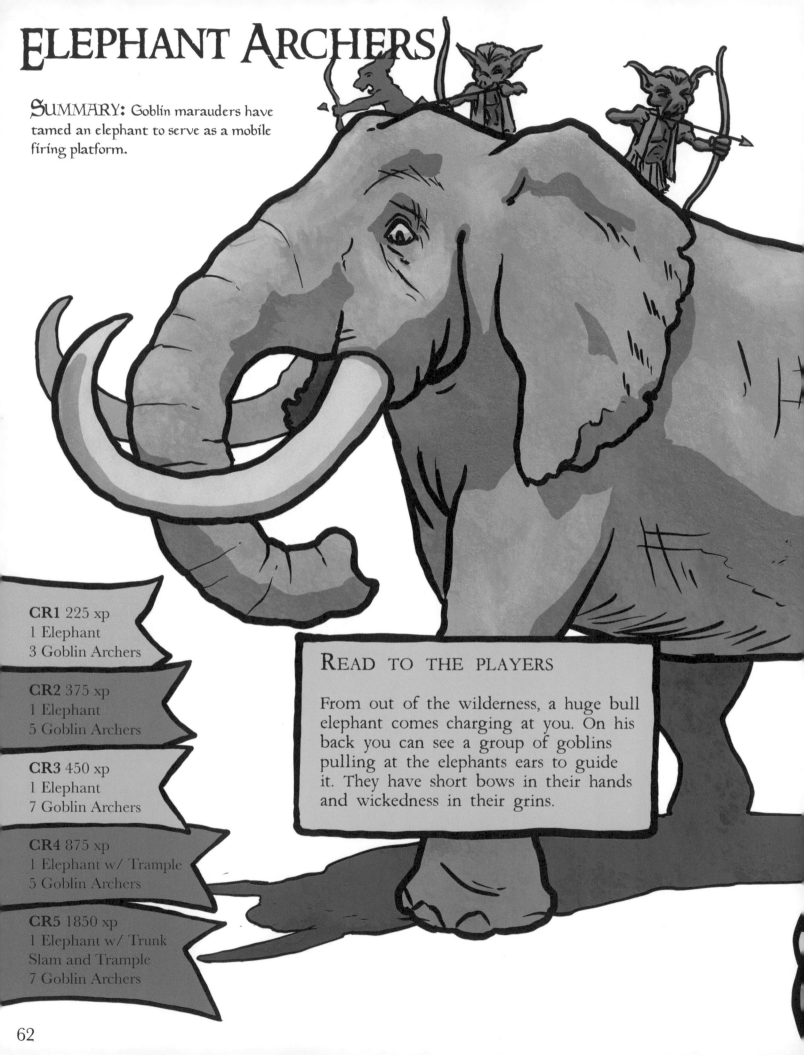

CR1 225 xp
1 Elephant
3 Goblin Archers

CR2 375 xp
1 Elephant
5 Goblin Archers

CR3 450 xp
1 Elephant
7 Goblin Archers

CR4 875 xp
1 Elephant w/ Trample
5 Goblin Archers

CR5 1850 xp
1 Elephant w/ Trunk
Slam and Trample
7 Goblin Archers

READ TO THE PLAYERS

From out of the wilderness, a huge bull elephant comes charging at you. On his back you can see a group of goblins pulling at the elephants ears to guide it. They have short bows in their hands and wickedness in their grins.

COMBAT

Rounds 1,2,3: One goblin guides the elephant and the others shoot arrows. The elephant uses only what offensive abilities are allowed by the CR.

Round 4: The elephant picks up a dead goblin and lobs it up to 30 feet at a PC. +7 to hit, 1d6+4 damage. Goblin archers continue to shoot.

Rounds 5+: The elephant has had enough. He shakes off any remaining goblins and lumbers away. At CR 4 & 5, he will fight to the death if further provoked.

GOBLIN ARCHER   CR 1/4 (50xp)

Small humanoid (goblinoid), neutral evil

Armor Class 13 (15 with cover) (leather armor)
Hit Points 7 (2d6)   **Speed** 30 ft.

STR	DEX	CON	INT	WIS	CHA
9 (-1)	14 (+2)	11 (+0)	9 (-1)	8 (-1)	7 (-2)

Skills Animal handling +2
Senses Darkvision 60 ft., passive Perception 9
Languages Common, Goblin

Crouching Cover. Each time a goblin archer shoots, it can use a bonus action to crouch down on the elephant's back, providing half cover against ranged attacks (+2 AC).

ACTIONS

Shortbow. Ranged Weapon Attack: +4 to hit, range 80/320 ft., one target. Hit: 5 (1d6 + 2) piercing damage

Bite. Melee Weapon Attack: +4 to hit, reach 5 ft., one creature. Hit: 1 (1d4 - 1) piercing damage.

RIDING ELEPHANT

Huge beast, unaligned   CR 4 (1100xp)

Armor Class 13 (natural armor)
Hit Points 95 (10d12+30)   Speed 40 ft.

STR	DEX	CON	INT	WIS	CHA
23 (+6)	9 (-1)	17 (+3)	3 (-4)	12 (+1)	6 (-2)

Senses passive Perception 11
Languages –

Trample (CR4 & CR5 only). The elephant can pass through the space of any creature size large or smaller. When the elephant passes through their space, creatures suffer 2d10 bludgeoning damage and are knocked prone. If they make a DC 12 Dexterity saving throw, they suffer only half damage and avoid being prone.

ACTIONS

Trunk slam(CR5 only). Melee Weapon Attack: +8 to hit, reach 5 ft., one target. Hit: 10 (1d8+6) bludgeoning damage and DC 13 Strength saving throw or be knocked prone.

TREASURE & RESOLUTION

Each goblin body has a poor quality shortbow and 1d4 arrows. The elephant, if killed, has tusks that can be harvested for up to 200 pounds of ivory and sold for 2 sp per pound.

TRADING TREE

SUMMARY: A quirky treant is eager to trade goods with the party.

READ TO THE PLAYERS

You notice a tree cluttered with stuff. Every limb and crook is laden with chests, crates, bags, and barrels. As you approach this most unusual sight, the tree rotates until a gnarled face appears and smiles at you.

In a deep, slow voice the tree says, "Gree-eet-ings. I-ee ammm Ell-mm-ore. Woo-ood you lie-kah to-ooh trr-aye-duh?"

You can show the illustration on the opposite page.

ELMORE

Elmore trades for quantity, not quality. For example, he will take two story books for one spell book, or two short swords for one greatsword. He might even have a few magical items among his wares, but does not place any higher value on them. He always gives things a vigorous shake to see if they fall apart because he doesn't want junk.

Elmore has no interest in coins or jewels and is incapable of thinking in terms of currency value. Nor is he interested in potions, liquids, or anything smaller than fist-sized because he has trouble holding them with his enormous fingers.

ELDORE THE TREANT
Huge plant, neutral   CR 9 (5,000 XP)

Armor Class 16 (natural armor)
Hit Points 140 (12d12 + 60)
Speed 30 ft.

STR	DEX	CON	INT	WIS	CHA
23 (+6)	9 (-1)	20 (+5)	13 (+1)	17 (+3)	13 (+1)

Skills Insight +8, Perception +8, History +6
Damage Resistances bludgeoning, piercing
Damage Vulnerabilities fire
Senses passive Perception 13
Languages Sylvan, Common, Elvish, Druidic

Spellcasting. Eldore can cast the following spells at will using wisdom as his casting ability; Detect Magic, Identify, Comprehend Languages, Sleep, Detect Magic

ACTIONS
Multiattack. The treant makes two slam attacks.

Slam. Melee Weapon Attack: +10 to hit, reach 10 ft., one target. Hit: 16 (3d6+6) bludgeoning damage.

WHAT DOES HE HAVE?

Anything the players ask about is possibly among Elmore's collection. Players can roll a d100 for each type of thing they inquire about.

01-08 Elmore has one and it is magical.
09-39 He has at least a dozen of them.
40-84 He has one.
85+ Elmore has none of those items.
99+ He is done trading for now and wanders off, deep in thought.

PRECARIOUS PASSAGE

SUMMARY: A narrow ledge is blocked by an elderly mountain goat who won't budge.

CR1 200xp
DC 11
30 ft. drop

CR2 300 xp
DC 12
50 ft. drop

CR3 450 xp
DC 13
60 ft. drop

CR4 650 xp
DC 14
70 ft. drop

CR5 900 xp
DC 15
80 ft. drop

READ TO THE PLAYERS

Your journey takes you across the face of a cliff. A narrow ledge, just barely wide enough for a person, is your only path. Careful footing and concentration are necessary to keep from plummeting to the depths below.

Half-way across now, walking single-file, you round a corner only to discover an obstacle. The ledge is blocked by a large, elderly mountain goat who is resting comfortably. He is not frightened by your presence and gives no indication that he wants to move.

Small fissures and handholds in the cliff face could be used to climb over and past the goat, though it is treacherous.

The Goat Problem

The players will undoubtedly come up with some innovative solutions to this dilemma. The DC for all skill checks and saving throws needed are listed in the CR chart above. Below are some additional guidelines to help you run this encounter:

Establish the marching order right away. PCs can switch places if both make an Acrobatics check. Failure means they must make Dexterity saves or fall.

PCs can attempt to climb using Athletics checks. Two checks are needed to bypass the goat. Failure means no progress is made. A critical failure means falling unless a Dexterity save is made.

Falling damage is 1d6 per 10 feet. (See CR chart above)

The goat is old and stubborn. He cannot be persuaded through Animal Handling. If provoked in any way he will use his ram attack.

Once the goat is down to half his health, he will leave, effortlessly bounding up the cliff face.

Treasure & Resolution

The goat has survived attacks in the past. In fact, he has two magic arrow heads beneath his hide which have healed over. If extracted, they will be discovered to be +2 silvered arrow heads which could be affixed to new arrows by a fletcher.

Grand Mountain Goat

Large beast, unaligned   CR 1 (200xp)

Armor Class 11 (natural armor)
Hit Points 45 (6d10+12) Speed 40 ft., Climb 30ft.

STR	DEX	CON	INT	WIS	CHA
19 (+4)	11 (+0)	14 (+2)	2 (-4)	14 (+2)	6 (-2)

Damage resistances cold
Senses passive Perception 12
Languages –

Sure-Footed. The goat has advantage on rolls to resist effects that would move it or knock it prone.

Actions

Ram. Melee Weapon Attack: +7 to hit, reach 5 ft., one target. Hit: 9 (2d4+4) bludgeoning damage and Strength saving throw or be knocked prone. Critically failing this save means being knocked off the cliff.

DUNES OF DELUSION

SUMMARY: Sand serpents lure the party into an ambush.

READ TO THE PLAYERS

Not only are the sun's rays scalding you from above, they are reflecting off the sand beneath you, as well. A hot wind shoots over the dunes, sending a spray of shimmering sand into the air, adding one more thing to guard your eyes against. As the granules shower down in front of you, a small oasis appears, revealed as if by magic. A sanctuary of green grasses and small shrubs encircle a small, refreshing little pond.

Springing the trap

The oasis is a sand serpent illusion designed to lure creatures into an ambush. Within the oasis the heads of sand serpents are peeking out, masked by illusory bushes. When the party is close enough, the serpents strike. Before they strike, have each player roll INT(investigation) DC 12. Characters who succeed realize that the oasis is an illusion and become alert just at the moment the trap is sprung. Those who fail the check are surprised. The sand here is deep and soft so movement for the PCs is halved.

CR1 500 xp
2 Sand Serpents

CR2 900 xp
3 Sand Serpents

CR3 1200 xp
4 Sand Serpents

CR4 1500 xp
5 Sand Serpents

CR5 2800 xp
8 Sand Serpents

COMBAT

Round 1(surprise): One serpent uses their Prismatic Breath, trying to catch as many PCs as it can in the 15-foot cone. Meanwhile any remaining serpents make bite attacks.

Round 2: Another serpent uses its breath weapon. Other serpents make bite attacks, as evenly distributed amongst the party as possible.

Round 3: If there are any serpents who have not used their breath weapon yet, they use it now, but recklessly. The serpents are not immune to each other's breath and must also save each time they are caught in a cone.

Round 4: Any serpent who has taken 7 or more damage flees on this round, burrowing into the sand and possibly provoking an opportunity attack. The remaining serpents make bite attacks.

Rounds 5+: The remaining serpents continue their bite attacks until the fight is over.

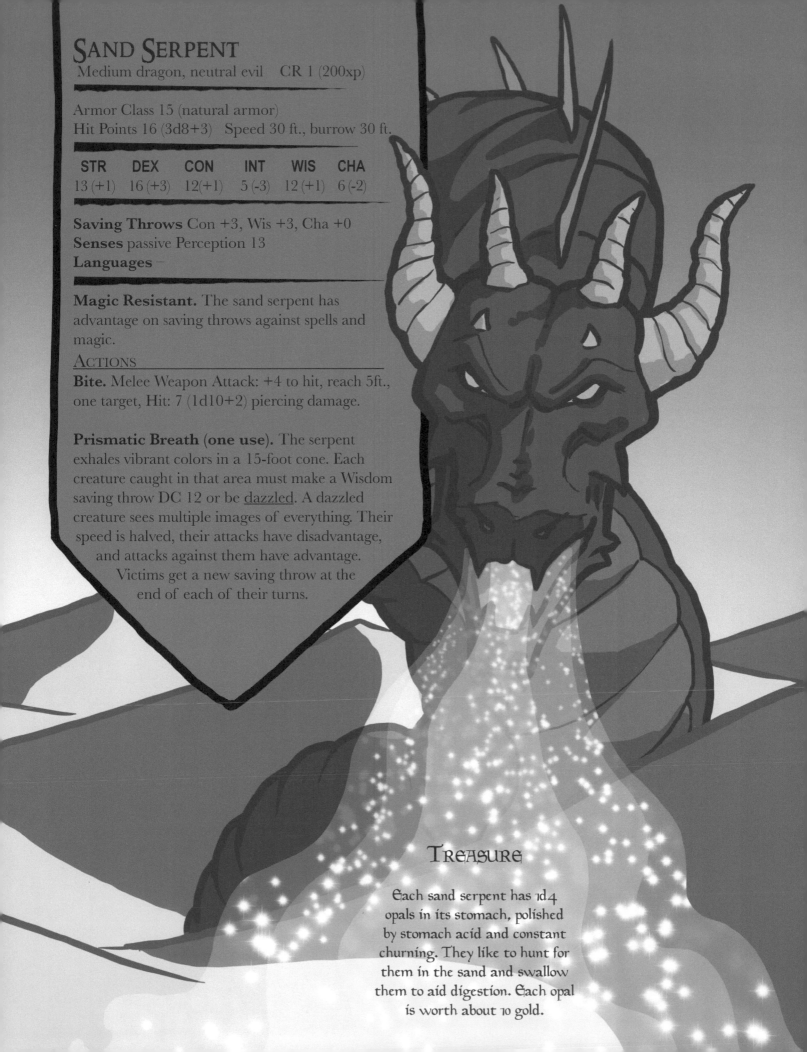

Sand Serpent

Medium dragon, neutral evil   CR 1 (200xp)

Armor Class 15 (natural armor)
Hit Points 16 (3d8+3)   Speed 30 ft., burrow 30 ft.

STR	DEX	CON	INT	WIS	CHA
13 (+1)	16 (+3)	12 (+1)	5 (-3)	12 (+1)	6 (-2)

Saving Throws Con +3, Wis +3, Cha +0
Senses passive Perception 13
Languages –

Magic Resistant. The sand serpent has advantage on saving throws against spells and magic.

ACTIONS

Bite. Melee Weapon Attack: +4 to hit, reach 5ft., one target, Hit: 7 (1d10+2) piercing damage.

Prismatic Breath (one use). The serpent exhales vibrant colors in a 15-foot cone. Each creature caught in that area must make a Wisdom saving throw DC 12 or be <u>dazzled</u>. A dazzled creature sees multiple images of everything. Their speed is halved, their attacks have disadvantage, and attacks against them have advantage.
Victims get a new saving throw at the end of each of their turns.

TREASURE

Each sand serpent has 1d4 opals in its stomach, polished by stomach acid and constant churning. They like to hunt for them in the sand and swallow them to aid digestion. Each opal is worth about 10 gold.

PICTURE PERFECT

SUMMARY: A dilettante wants the party to pose for his painting.

READ TO THE PLAYERS

While passing across a meadow, you see a small camp. There is single tent bearing a noble pennant and two soldiers. Nearby a middle-aged man, stripped to the waist, leans on an artist's easel and paints intently.

Upon seeing you, the artist gestures eagerly for you to approach.

If the PCs avoid the camp, this encounter is over, but if they approach, continue reading.

"Hail, travelers! Your arrival is an unexpected blessing! I am Lord Whitebridge, perhaps you have heard of me, or seen my portrait of the Queen? No matter. I have been out here all day trying to capture the beauty of this meadow and failing miserably, MISERABLY! But just now, as you were walking through, I realized YOU are what has been missing from my scene! Please, if you would pose for me, I will make it worth your while."

IF INTERESTED, ONE PC NEGOTIATES THE PRICE AND HOW LONG THEY WILL POSE.

Roll CHA(persuasion) DC14

✓

"Very well," says Lord Whitebridge, "I agree to your terms. I will pay you each 20 gold apiece if you'll pose for two hours."

✗

"Very well," says Lord Whitebridge, "I agree to your terms. I will pay you each 10 gold apiece if you'll pose for three hours."

He arranges the party about twenty feet away from his easel, each in a heroic pose standing in the tall grass.

"Come now," he says. "You can look more heroic than that."

EACH PLAYER ROLLS CHA(performance) DC14

The characters who succeed are praised by His Lordship, but actually put themselves in a more challenging pose and they will be at disadvantage for the following Constitution saving throws.

"Now hold very still!"

Each player must roll 2 or 3 Constitution saving throws DC10 (1 per hour). If they fail a save, they are scolded by Lord Whitebridge and they are at disadvantage on the next save. Anyone who fails two saves finds it impossible to hold their pose and is asked to leave, getting only a single gold coin for their time.

LORD WHITEBRIDGE CR 3 (700xp)
Medium humanoid (any race), chaotic neutral

Armor Class 16 (Chainmail Armor)
Hit Points: 22 (5d6+5) **Speed** 30 ft.

STR	DEX	CON	INT	WIS	CHA
12 (+1)	13 (+1)	12 (+1)	12 (+1)	11 (+1)	15 (+2)

Senses passive Perception 13
Languages Common, Elven, Draconic

Spellcasting. Gerund is a 5th-level sorcerer. His spellcasting ability is Charisma (spell save DC 13) His preferred spells are **bolded**.

Cantrips (at will): Light, Mage Hand, Message

1st level (4 slots): Charm Person, **Sleep**

2nd level (3 slots): **Hold Person**, Misty Step

3rd level (2 slots): Hypnotic Pattern

ACTIONS

Dagger. Melee Weapon Attack: +3 to hit, reach 5 ft., one target. Hit: 3 (1d4 +1) piercing damage.

MEN AT ARMS CR 3 (700xp)
Medium humanoid (any race), lawful neutral

Armor Class 17 (splint)
Hit Points 58 (9d8+18) **Speed** 30 ft.

STR	DEX	CON	INT	WIS	CHA
16 (+3)	12 (+1)	15 (+2)	10 (+0)	12 (+1)	10 (+0)

Skills Athletics +5, Perception +3, Insight +3
Senses passive Perception 13
Languages Common plus one other

ACTIONS

Multiattack. The man at arms may make two melee attacks.

Longsword. Melee Weapon Attack: +6 to hit, reach 5 ft., one target. Hit: 8 (1d10 + 3) slashing damage.

Heavy Crossbow. Ranged Weapon Attack: +4 to hit, range 100/400 ft., one target. Hit: 5 (1d10 + 1) piercing damage.

RESOLUTIONS

1. IF EVERYONE POSES UNTIL THE END:
Lord Whitebridge is thrilled with the result of the painting and invites the party to his home for dinner. He will offer helpful insights into their current quest(s).

2. IF ONLY ONE PC POSES 'TIL THE END:
Lord Whitebridge is not happy with the result, even though it is an extraordinarily beautiful portrait of the PC. He boxes up the painting, gives it to the PC, and bids them all farewell.

3. IF NEITHER OF THE ABOVE RESULTS HAPPEN:
Lord Whitebridge is unhappy with the result. He flings the canvas into the meadow and storms into his tent. The men at arms ensure everyone is paid appropriately.

COMPETITIVE PIE FILLING

SUMMARY: An annual holiday features a baking contest and a competitive eating contest.

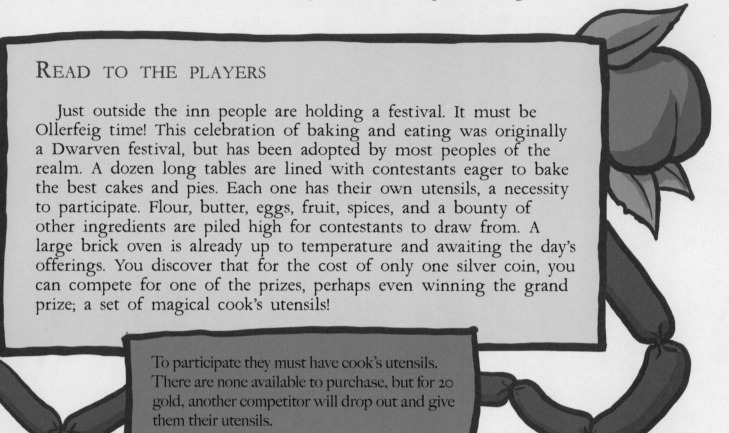

READ TO THE PLAYERS

Just outside the inn people are holding a festival. It must be Ollerfeig time! This celebration of baking and eating was originally a Dwarven festival, but has been adopted by most peoples of the realm. A dozen long tables are lined with contestants eager to bake the best cakes and pies. Each one has their own utensils, a necessity to participate. Flour, butter, eggs, fruit, spices, and a bounty of other ingredients are piled high for contestants to draw from. A large brick oven is already up to temperature and awaiting the day's offerings. You discover that for the cost of only one silver coin, you can compete for one of the prizes, perhaps even winning the grand prize; a set of magical cook's utensils!

To participate they must have cook's utensils. There are none available to purchase, but for 20 gold, another competitor will drop out and give them their utensils.

After two hours all the baked goods are finished and cooled. Participants need to name their creation. The judges taste the results and award the winners. The player(s) make their check and, if their result is higher than 15, replace one of the contestants listed below.

DC 16: 3rd place, Boviene Gilderspoon, "Boviene's Dragonsberry Upsidedown Cake", awarded a cask of Rook's Abbey spiced rum.

DC 17: 2nd place, Hobford Innskeep, "Bell Tower Inn Apple Pie", awarded a brick of Flindril's Wondrous Ice, (A 2 lb. brick of cloudy grey quartz that always remains ice cold. No attunement required. If subjected to an intense heat source, the brick shatters.)

DC 18: 1st place, Hatheagen Runesbrook, "Figgy Persimmon Tort Cake", awarded the enchanted cooks utensils. (The magical utensils prevent cooking food from sticking or burning, granting you advantage on cook's utensils checks. No attunement required.)

Participants will roll 3 Constitution saving throws, one every ten minutes. The check result is how many pies they consumed during that span of time. If they get above 12 they are doing well, but below 10 they are losing ground to the other competitors. If any of the PCs critically fumble, they vomit and are disqualified. Six of the other two dozen competitors throw up during the last ten minutes.

The three saving throws are totaled up to find the winner. The highest npc total is 39. If none of the PCs beat 39 then chubby young Morris Morrisson wins the competition.

In the event of a tie, the winner is decided by crowd applause. Roll CHA(performance) checks.

Games and More Games

Summary: A simple pub game turns into a whodunit murder mystery.

The Set-up

While in a very tiny pub, a game of pitch pot breaks out. To play pitch pot, players stand ten feet away from a clay pot and take turns tossing arrows into it.

The party is invited to nominate someone to play against Gandry, the local champ. Make the players think this is the goal of the encounter.

While they are playing, be sure to describe how people are moving around and bumping into each other in the tiny pub.

The player takes their 5 tosses first, trying to make a DC of 16. They can roll their choice of DEX(acrobatics) or DEX(sleight of hand). Gandry makes his 5 tosses next. He has a +5 bonus to his tosses.

The crowd cheers as soon as a winner becomes clear and then everyone squeezes around trying to get back to their drinks.

Read to the players

A woman's scream suddenly draws everyone's attention back to Gandry who is slumped against the wall. The sheriff, a large, bearded fellow, rushes over and declares the man has been stabbed to death.

"Them strangers must've done it!" yells one of the patrons.

"Now don't start pointing fingers at them," says the sheriff. "I've been keeping an eye on those strangers all night and I don't believe they are to blame. Someone else here is a murderer and no one is leaving until I find out who!"

The sheriff comes over to you and says, "Do us both a favor. Put your heads together and see if you can come up with anything that will help me. I'm going to start interviewing everyone."

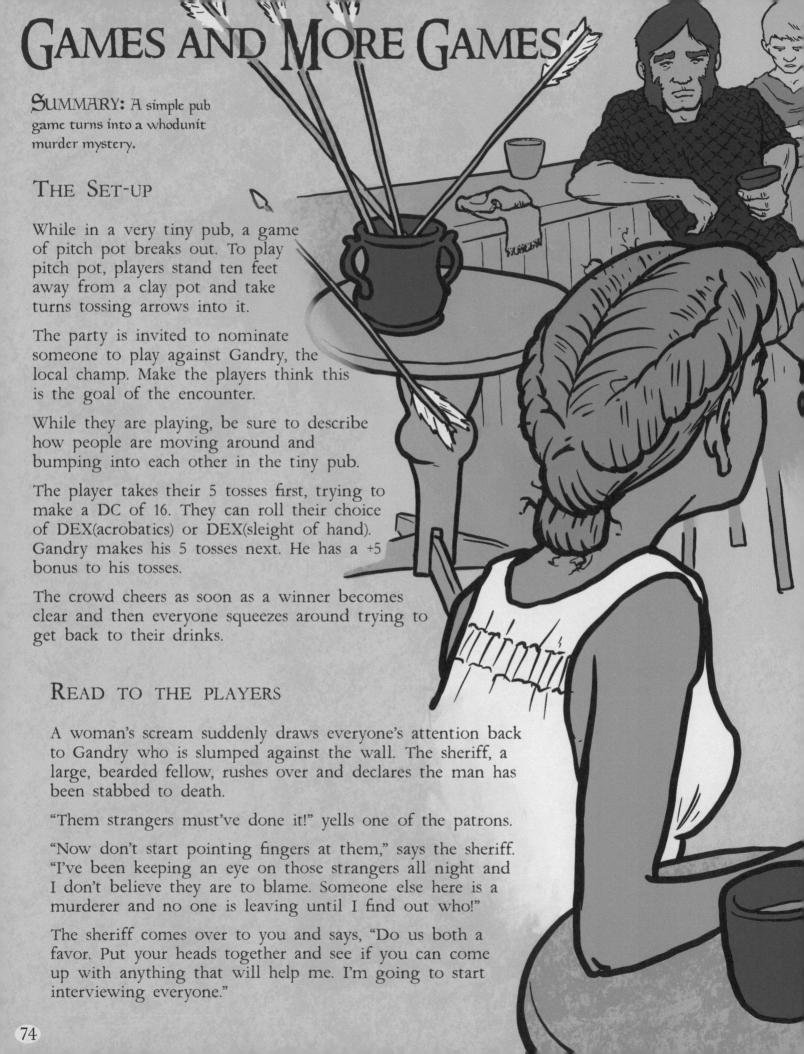

GETTING TO THE TRUTH

Only one roll should be made for the following skill checks. A second character can aid ONLY if they are proficient in the skill check being used and rolls a check of 12 or higher. If successful, they enable the person making the check to roll with advantage.

Each of the checks will help the players to establish which of the seven possible suspects had the means, the motive, and the opportunity to kill Gandry the glassblower. Read all the clues for which they achieve the DC for.

After all the checks are made, they must make their best guess who the real culprit is and present their case to the sheriff. The suspects are not open to questioning by the PCs. The players must rely on the evidence they have at hand while the sheriff conducts his own investigation.

Here are the 7 possible suspects: Silas the smith, Colandra the cook, Thella the thatcher, Melindra the serving maid, Fendric the forester, Bayford the bartender, Ernie the herbalist

INT(religion):

DC 12: Bayford the bartender is tattooed with the symbol of a pacifist sect whose members swear off violence of any kind.
DC 16: During the match, when Gandry cursed the gods after a missed shot, both Colandra the cook and Ernie the herbalist were offended and made counter curses with their fingers.

WIS(perception):

DC 12: Colandra the cook was flirting with both Gandry and Fendric the forester.
DC 16: You remember seeing Silas going through Thella the thatcher's bag.

WIS(insight):

DC 12: Things between Silas the smith and Thella the thatcher are very tense.
DC 16: Bayford the bartender appears to be in love with Colandra the cook, but she scorns his advances.

WIS(medicine):

DC 12: The entry wound was round, not flat like a blade.
DC 16: Melindra, Thella, and Ernie all lack the strength to puncture through Gandry's jacket and his back and rib muscles.
DC 19: Thella the thatcher is in the early stages of pregnancy.

INT(investigation):

DC 12: Colandra the cook's outfit was so sparse there would be nowhere to conceal a weapon.
DC 16: Fendric the forester has mud on his boots. There is no trace of mud on the floor near where Gandry stood.

INT(history):

DC 12: Melindra the serving maid is wearing the tartan pattern of the Highvale clan who are in a land dispute with Gandry's clan, the Danvricks.
DC 16: A thatching needle, used to sew bundles of thatch into place, would perfectly match the diameter of Gandry's wound.

WHAT REALLY HAPPENED

Silas and Thella were in love. Silas was going to ask Thella to marry him. Thella told him she is pregnant with Gandry's baby. Silas took Thella's thatching needle from her bag and used it to stab Gandry, then he slipped it back into her bag.

TREASURE & RESOLUTION

If they guess correctly and accuse Silas, he confesses and pronounces his hated for Gandry and Thella. The sheriff rewards them with 10 gold x their total level, and perhaps another quest.

If they guess incorrectly, or fail to guess at all, they are ridiculed by the sheriff as wanna-be heroes with no common sense.

Lucky Suckers

Summary: A shire of halflings, down on their luck, made a pact with a demon. Their luck is now extraordinary, but also, never enough. Focused only on attaining more, they now steal luck from others.

CR1 250 xp
2 Luck Suckers

CR2 450 xp
3 Luck Suckers

CR3 600 xp
4 Luck Suckers

CR4 900 xp
6 Luck Suckers

CR5 1750 xp
10 Luck Suckers

Read to the Players

Your path takes you into an area that you don't immediately recognize as a town. This halfling shire is so neglected and overgrown that it blends in with the nature around it. Judging by the state of it, you would guess this place was abandoned twenty or thirty years ago, which makes it all the more surprising when filthy halflings emerge from hiding places to attack you.

Combat

Round 1 (surprise): Any character with a passive perception less than 16 is surprised this round and cannot take actions. The halfling luck suckers emerge from various hiding places and attack with bare hands. They try to slam their fists into their target to drain their luck (see Sucker Punch action).

Round 2: The halflings begin trying to lure the PCs into a trap. They make an attack and then strategically move, provoking an opportunity attack. A 5x10 pit trap is concealed by branches and leaves. Though hard to see, the halflings know exactly where it is located. The first PC to step into the 5x10 area falls into the pit. They can attempt a DC 15 Dexterity saving throw. If they succeed, they have grabbed onto a tree root at the edge of the pit and are restrained until the start of their next turn. If the saving throw fails, they fall 20 feet to the bottom of the pit and into waist-deep mud. The pit's walls are soft earth. The Athletics check to climb out is DC 15.

Rounds 3+: The halflings continue to make punching attacks and throw any unconscious victims into the pit.

Luck Sucker CR 1/2 (100xp)
Medium humanoid (halfling), chaotic evil

Armor Class 12
Hit Points 17 (3d6+6) **Speed** 25 ft.

STR	DEX	CON	INT	WIS	CHA
10 (+0)	14 (+2)	14 (+2)	11 (+0)	9 (-1)	12 (+1)

Skills Stealth +6, Perception +2
Senses Darkvision 60 ft., passive Perception 12
Languages Common, Halfling

Damned Lucky. The halfling has advantage to all attack rolls, saving throws, and ability checks. In addition, they reroll all natural 1s.

Actions

Sucker Punch. Melee Weapon Attack: +4 to hit, reach 5 ft., one creature. Hit: 2 (1d4) bludgeoning damage and the target must make a DC 14 Charisma saving throw. On a failed save, the victim feels unlucky and suffers disadvantage on all attack rolls, saving throws, and ability checks for 1 round.

Treasure & Resolution

The shire has little of value in it. There is written evidence of how the shire fell on hard times many years ago and all the residents were forced to sell off their possessions. In desperation they turned to a demon of luck who promised to end their string of misfortunes. Their luck changed, but so did their desires. They lost all interest in family, farming, and food. Only luck could sate their hunger. All but these few have died. In the homes, skeletal remains still lay in beds.

One of the halflings wears a black cat's paw as an amulet.

    Amulet of Perseverance: Whenever the wearer rolls a 1 on an attack or saving throw, they gain 10 temporary hit points lasting up to 1 hour. Requires attunement.

ONLY GAME IN TOWN

SUMMARY: There's only one merchant in the town who sells what the party is after. Unfortunately, he's addicted to high stakes games of chance.

READ TO THE PLAYERS

There's only one place in town that sells what you're looking for; Tartaron's Fine Goods. The proprietor, a thickly bearded tiefling, is sitting at a table playing dice with another customer. "I'll be right with you," he calls out. "We're just finishing up this game."

A few minutes later, the customer throws up his fists in victory, grabs the coins and the goods from the table, and hurries out the door.

"Can't win 'em all," says the proprietor. "My name's Tartaron. Welcome. Now, what can I help you find?"

Tartaron's Fine Goods sells precisely the items the adventurers are looking for. If they ask about pricing, Tartaron will tell them what he thinks they are worth. He won't just trade coins for goods, though. He is addicted to the thrill of the game.

Tartaron will first negotiate a price for what the PC wants to purchase. Then he will insist that they play a game for it. He stakes the item and they stake the money or equivalent goods. Winner takes all. He will even let them pick the game; Dice, Dragonchess, Three Dragon Ante, or Cards.

Proficient in all four gaming sets, Tartaron gets a +3 bonus to his gaming checks.

CHEATING

Tartaron is no novice. He has seen all the tricks over the years and is always expecting someone to cheat. He has advantage on Insight and Perception checks to detect cheating. If caught, he will eject them from his shop and refuse to do business with them again.

SISTER STRIPE

SUMMARY: A baby tiger is dying and neither the mother nor her human companion know what to do.

READ TO THE PLAYERS

Deep in the wilderness, you hear a sound that sends a chill down your spine. It is the deep rumbling voice of a big cat. Not a roar, but a warning that you are getting too close.

If the PCs avoid the sound, this encounter is over, but if they approach, continue reading.

A uniquely beautiful sight greets your eyes. A young woman, a warrior by her appearance, is riding on the back of a tiger. She is holding a newborn cub in her arms. The woman looks at you with concern and on the verge of tears. The little tiger cub looks very ill.

The Challenge

The woman and the tiger have been together since birth. The woman, born deaf, and the tiger, born blind, were raised together like sisters and are dependent upon each other for survival. Right now both are desperately concerned for the health of the cub, desperate enough to beseech strangers for help.

The PCs may come up with a variety of ways to help. Below are some useful skill and tool checks that they could employ.

THE CUB:
INT(medicine) DC 10: The newborn cub is malnourished. It isn't ready to eat solid foods and needs milk.

THE TIGER:
To inspect the tigress they first need a WIS(animal handling) DC 15 but they get advantage since the young woman is aiding them.

INT(medicine) DC 12: She is old for a tiger and, though she managed to give birth one last time, she is not producing milk. However, a certain combination of herbs may be able to induce milk production in the tigress.

HERBALISM KIT check:
• Less than 12: The herbs fail. They make the tigress vomit.
• 12 to 15: The herbs work and in a couple hours the tigress begins producing milk. However, she suffers stabbing abdominal pain and becomes dangerous to be around.
• More than 15: The herbs work and without any side effects. In a few hours she is making milk.

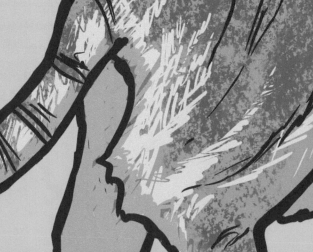
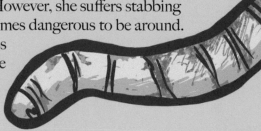

Treasure & Resolution

If they were UNABLE to help the cub, the sisters wander away. However, if the party was indeed able to help, then the sisters are pleased. They will lead the party back to their home, an old but sturdy stone cottage hidden away in the wilderness. There are chickens running about and animal hides hanging on stretchers. It becomes obvious that the woman tans the hides of animals that they hunt and that she then makes goods from the leather. She shows them a multitude of various items that she has made and urges them each to take one. Her leatherwork goods are exceptionally well made and decorated with feathers, fur, colorful stones, and wooden beads. They include: bracers, shoes & boots, bags & purses, belts, hats, scabbards, slings, and other such items. She does not have large items like pants, coats, or armor. Once they choose an item, the sisters send them away. They are excited to return to the job of raising the new cub.

Alchemically Locked

Summary: highwaymen attack an alchemist, resulting in an accidental explosion and dire consequences.

Read to the Players

You hear a series of faint booms like distant thunder. Some minutes later on your journey you happen upon the source of that sound. A donkey-drawn cart overturned into a ravine, you assume as the result of a bandit attack because there are dead bodies scattered about. The contents of the wagon apparently had exploded. Shattered glassware is embedded in the trees, and in the ground, and in the bodies. An acrid smell permeates the area. The bodies are discolored, bulging and pulsing with what appears to be alchemical activity. Without warning, the men leap to their feet in a chemical rage and begin violently flailing their fists at you!

Useful Skill Check

INT(alchemical supplies) DC 12: These people are alchemically active so dousing them with antitoxin may help neutralize them.

Hitting a Toxic Terror with a vial of antitoxin gives it disadvantage for 1 minute, no save. A second vial will render it unconscious.

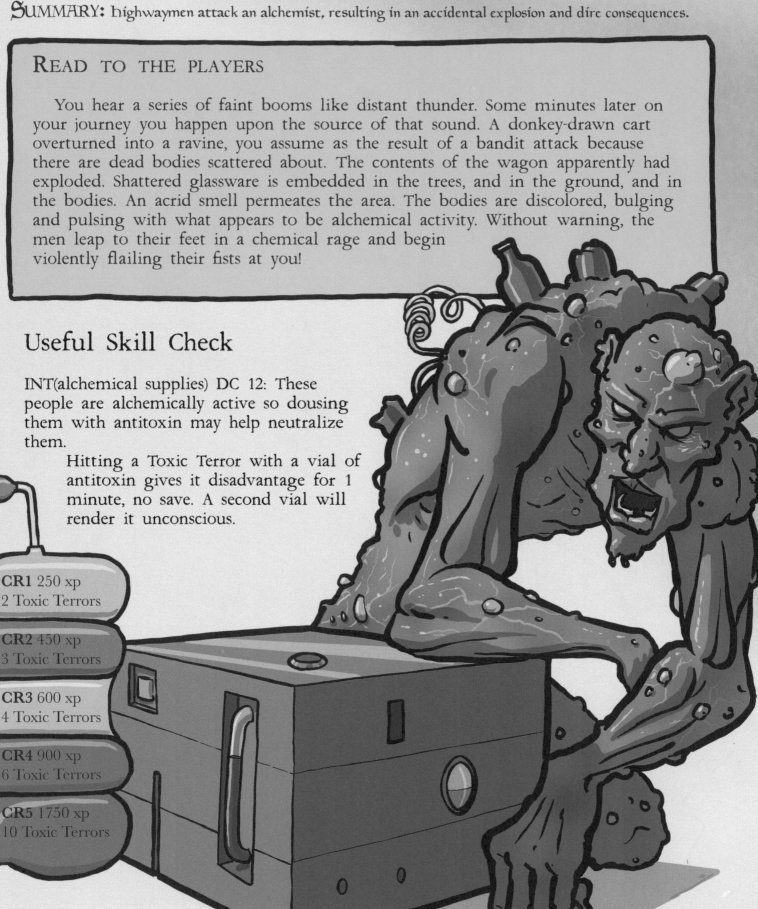

CR1 250 xp
2 Toxic Terrors

CR2 450 xp
3 Toxic Terrors

CR3 600 xp
4 Toxic Terrors

CR4 900 xp
6 Toxic Terrors

CR5 1750 xp
10 Toxic Terrors

COMBAT

Round 1: The Toxic Terrors leap into melee with the PCs and attempt slam attacks.

Round 2: One of the terrors belches. It spends the entire round belching out a noxious, green cloud. The others make slam attacks.

> The belched cloud covers a 20x20 area.. Characters who begin their turn within the cloud become poisoned unless they make a Constitution saving throw DC 13. If a poisoned character starts their turn outside the cloud, they get a new save to end the effect. The terrors are immune.

Round 3: The donkey stands up. It is also peppered with broken glass and covered with pulsing green sores. The donkey staggers into the melee but is not aggressive. The terrors ignore it and continue making slam attacks.

Round 4: While the terrors continue their mindless attacks, the donkey is inflating. Odd bulges appear all around its body.

Round 5: The terrors make their attacks and then the donkey explodes! All creatures in 30 feet of the donkey take 2d4 thunder damage. A new 30x30 noxious green cloud occupies the space with the same properties as the other one.

Rounds 6+: The terrors continue their attacks until one side wins.

TOXIC TERROR CR 1/2 (100xp)
Medium monstrosity, chaotic evil

Armor Class 12
Hit Points 25 (3d10+9)   **Speed** 30 ft.

STR	DEX	CON	INT	WIS	CHA
18 (+4)	14 (+2)	16 (+3)	2 (-4)	2 (-4)	2 (-4)

Skills Perception +1
Condition Immunities charmed, frightened
Damage Resistances acid, fire, lightning
Senses passive Perception 11
Languages —

Spewing Wounds. When hit with a slashing or piercing attack, stinging fluid ejects from the wound. Anyone within 5 ft. gets a Dexterity save DC 14 to avoid taking 1d4 acid damage.

ACTIONS

Slam. Melee Weapon Attack: +6 to hit, reach 5 ft., one target. 6 (1d4+4) bludgeoning damage.

TREASURE & RESOLUTION

The only thing that survived the explosion intact was a large brass cube. It has various glass windows in it that display liquids of different colors and there is a funnel-like opening on top.

INT(investigation) DC 14: This is a locked container and the key is alchemical.

INT(alchemical supplies) DC 15: Read the alchemical instructions, mix up the appropriate key, and pour into the lock. The box bubbles and hisses and clicks and then opens. NOTE: If the wrong substance is poured into the lock, it simply drains out the bottom.

INT(thieves tools) DC 22: Trick the box into opening.

If the box is opened through force, the contents are destroyed with a powerful acid. Inside the box is a 1 foot cubic chamber that is currently holding a book of alchemical research and recipes. For someone proficient in Alchemical Supplies, having this book on hand increases their proficiency bonus by 4.

GRAPPLESTONE STREET

SUMMARY: A bizarre denizen of the city uses rats to terrorize a bakery.

READ TO THE PLAYERS

The warm, comforting smell of fresh bread hangs in the air as you walk down the cobblestone street. Up ahead, in the doorway of the bakery you see two people in a tense exchange. The baker is waving her rolling pin at a filthy beggar while shouting for him to leave her doorstep.

"Get away!" she yells. "I gave you a biscuit now go take your lunacy elsewhere! You are driving away customers!"

"The crumbs belong to us!" shouts the beggar, as dozens of rats swarm from the shadows and surround him. "We are taking the crumbs!"

The baker screams and retreats inside, as more and more rats begin to flood the area.

COMBAT

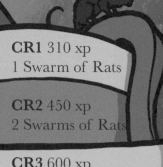

CR1 310 xp
1 Swarm of Rats

CR2 450 xp
2 Swarms of Rats

CR3 600 xp
4 Swarms of Rats

CR4 880 xp
7 Swarms of Rats

CR5 1700 xp
13 Swarms of Rats

Round 1: The beggar stands amid a swarm of rats. That swarm will move into the space of the first person to engage him with a melee weapon. If there are more swarms (see the CR chart), they attack whomever else is a threat in order of closeness. The beggar raises his hands up with wild fervor and the cobblestones of the street all begin to shake.

Rounds 2+: The rats will continue to attack whomever they originally chose as their target. The beggar's strange magic causes numerous cobblestones to elongate like snakes that grab at enemies within 50 feet of the beggar. Other snakes deflect attacks away from him, adding to his AC.

On the beggar's turn, the cobblestone snakes make grapple attempts against anyone in the area, even if they are already grappled. Anyone who is doubly grappled in this way becomes incapacitated and can take no physical actions aside from trying to escape the grapple. The snakes add +5 to their grapple checks.

Useful Skill Check

WIS(poisoner's kit) DC 14: A quick mixture of dried clover mold and flailstone dust, showered upon a swarm, will paralyze the rats instantly with twitching spasms until they eventually die from heart failure.

Treasure & Resolution

The baker, Eleanor, will reward the victors with fresh bread and pastries. The beggar, Twelve Toe Edgar, dissolves into a heap of dead rats. Inside this heap is a magic choker, made of woven rat hairs which grants the Keen Smell feature of the rats. Requires attunement.

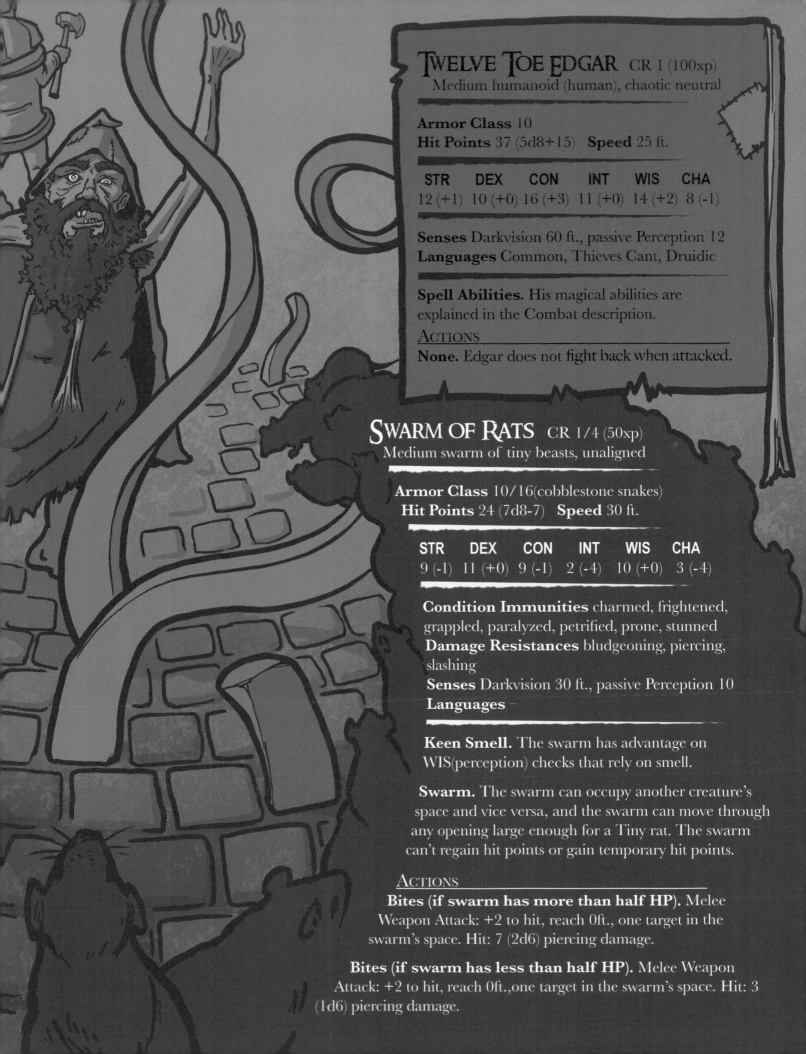

TWELVE TOE EDGAR CR 1 (100xp)
Medium humanoid (human), chaotic neutral

Armor Class 10
Hit Points 37 (5d8+15) **Speed** 25 ft.

STR	DEX	CON	INT	WIS	CHA
12 (+1)	10 (+0)	16 (+3)	11 (+0)	14 (+2)	8 (-1)

Senses Darkvision 60 ft., passive Perception 12
Languages Common, Thieves Cant, Druidic

Spell Abilities. His magical abilities are explained in the Combat description.

ACTIONS
None. Edgar does not fight back when attacked.

SWARM OF RATS CR 1/4 (50xp)
Medium swarm of tiny beasts, unaligned

Armor Class 10/16(cobblestone snakes)
Hit Points 24 (7d8-7) **Speed** 30 ft.

STR	DEX	CON	INT	WIS	CHA
9 (-1)	11 (+0)	9 (-1)	2 (-4)	10 (+0)	3 (-4)

Condition Immunities charmed, frightened, grappled, paralyzed, petrified, prone, stunned
Damage Resistances bludgeoning, piercing, slashing
Senses Darkvision 30 ft., passive Perception 10
Languages —

Keen Smell. The swarm has advantage on WIS(perception) checks that rely on smell.

Swarm. The swarm can occupy another creature's space and vice versa, and the swarm can move through any opening large enough for a Tiny rat. The swarm can't regain hit points or gain temporary hit points.

ACTIONS
Bites (if swarm has more than half HP). Melee Weapon Attack: +2 to hit, reach 0ft., one target in the swarm's space. Hit: 7 (2d6) piercing damage.

Bites (if swarm has less than half HP). Melee Weapon Attack: +2 to hit, reach 0ft.,one target in the swarm's space. Hit: 3 (1d6) piercing damage.

CIRCLING THE WEDDING HORSE

SUMMARY: Giant vultures circle in the sky above a horse that is trapped and soon to die.

CR1 500 xp	
2 Giant Vultures	

CR2 900 xp
3 Giant Vultures

CR3 1200 xp
4 Giant Vultures

CR4 1500 xp
5 Giant Vultures

CR5 2800 xp
8 Giant Vultures

READ TO THE PLAYERS

High up in the grey, overcast sky you see a group of vultures circling. They have their eyes on something to the east of you. At first they appear to be flying very low but you quickly realize they aren't low, they are huge! A whinny of distress tells you those giant vultures are circling a horse.

> If the PCs investigate further, continue reading, otherwise this encounter is concluded.

A horse, decorated for a wedding, is tangled up in young trees. The garlands of flowers, the reins, and other kit is all badly knotted. The horse is exhausted from trying to break free. Seeing you approach their prey, some of the giant vultures scream and dive down at you.

COMBAT

Round 1: The vultures were enjoying the suffering of the horse and will not tolerate anyone freeing it from its misery. Only the vultures indicated in the CR attack, the rest are too afraid.

The vultures go last in initiative. On their turn they land and make attacks against whichever PC is closest to the horse. Until their turn, though, they are in the air and out of range of melee attacks.

Round 2: Up to three vultures can attack a single target at a time. They prefer to dispatch enemies one at a time. If there are more than 3, the extras attack at whomever is furthest away from the horse, forcing the PCs to split ranks.

Round 3: The most wounded vulture panics, disengages, and flies away. The rest continue their attacks.

Round 4: Once again, the most wounded vulture in the fight disengages and flies away in a panic. The others, if there are any, keep fighting.

Round 5: The first vulture who flew away returns to the fight! It ands and attacks whomever seems least dangerous.

Rounds 6+: The vultures will continue to fight unless they are outnumbered. As soon as they are outnumbered, they will disengage and fly away.

GIANT VULTURE CR 1 (200xp)
Large beast, neutral evil

Armor Class 10
Hit Points 22 (3d10+6)   **Speed** 10 ft., fly 60 ft.

STR	DEX	CON	INT	WIS	CHA
15 (+2)	10 (+0)	15 (+2)	6 (-2)	12 (+1)	7 (-2)

Senses Darkvision 30 ft., passive Perception 10
Languages understands Common but can't speak

Keen Sight and Smell. The vulture has advantage on WIS(perception) checks that rely on sight or smell.

Pack Tactics. The vulture has advantage on an attack roll against a creature if at least one of the vulture's allies is within 5 feet of the creature.

ACTIONS
Multiattack. The vulture makes two attacks: one with its beak and one with its talons.

Beak. Melee Weapon Attack: +4 to hit, reach 5ft., one target, Hit: 7 (2d4+2) piercing damage.

Talons. Melee Weapon Attack: +4 to hit, reach 5ft., one target, Hit: 9 (2d6+2) piercing damage.

TREASURE & RESOLUTION

There is no sign of the bride and groom who belonged with this horse. By all appearances, it seems to have been trapped here for at least two days. It is draped with so many garlands, it is no wonder that it got tangled up. The horse requires some care but will make a full recovery. It has a full riding tack on and is further loaded down with the following: 100 feet of braided hemp rope (decorated with flowers), a 2-person tent, a basket filled with bread and cheese, two bottles of wine, a patchwork quilt, common men's and women's clothing, and cooking utensils.

GLOOM AND DARTING DOOM

SUMMARY: A mother's young child has wandered out onto giant lily pads and is now afraid to come back to shore. Time is critical as bloodthirsty birds are hunting.

READ TO THE PLAYERS

The shadows stretch long as the sun kisses the horizon. Up ahead you find a woman in distress at the edge of a large stagnant pond. At first glimpse she is startled by your appearance, but then hurries over to you, desperation written upon her face.

"Good people! My son, my son!" she cries. "He is only four years old! Help me, please! I cannot lose him! He crawled out on the lily pads and now is afraid to come back. Please hurry, the night birds are coming. I can already hear them!"

The pond has giant lily pads, each five feet in diameter. Upon one of these, far from the shore, sits a terrified little boy hugging his knees. A flock of birds is screaming across the twilight sky in your direction.

CR1 275 xp
4 lily pads away
6 Gloom Darts

CR2 450 xp
5 lily pads away
10 Gloom Darts

CR3 700 xp
6 lily pads away
14 Gloom Darts

CR4 1200 xp
7 lily pads away
19 Gloom Darts

CR5 1750 xp
8 lily pads away
28 Gloom Darts

The "Night Birds":
WIS(nature) DC 12: The birds are Gloom Darts, nocturnal birds the size of ravens. They hunt in packs, using spear-like beaks to dive bomb large prey. They are most likely to attack a creature who is moving.

Getting to the boy:
Swimming out to the boy is not possible. The network of giant lily pads obstructs movement. Walking on top of the lily pads is possible but hard. A DEX(acrobatics) check is required to traverse them. DC 14: leap to next lily pad. DC 18: scramble across two lily pads. Less than 14 means the lily pad sunk under their step and they couldn't move. On a natural 1, they fall in the water. STR(athletics) check DC 14 is required to climb back on.

COMBAT

Have the birds arrive when one or more characters are on the lily pads. Roll initiative. One trio of birds descends to attack each round. The rest weave about through the air and are fair game for ranged attacks.
    They swoop down in trios to gain advantage on their attacks. Choose a random target from among those moving on the lily pads. If no targets are available they attack a character on shore. Birds that hit their target will disengage and fly away the following round. Birds that miss their diving attack continue flying past, provoking an opportunity attack from the target.

GLOOM DARTS CR 1/8 (25xp)
Small beast, unaligned

Armor Class 10
Hit Points 7 (2d6) **Speed** 10 ft., fly 60 ft.

STR	DEX	CON	INT	WIS	CHA
6 (-2)	15 (+2)	11 (+0)	3 (-4)	14 (+2)	5 (-3)

Senses Darkvision 120 ft., passive Perception 14
Languages –

Keen Sight and Hearing. The gloom dart has advantage on WIS(perception) checks that rely on sight or hearing.

Pack Tactics. The gloom dart has advantage on an attack roll against a creature if at least one of the gloom dart's allies is within 5 feet of the creature.

ACTIONS
Beak. Melee Weapon Attack: +4 to hit, reach 5ft., one target, Hit: 4 (1d4+2) piercing damage.

TREASURE & RESOLUTION

The mother, Lucinda, will be incredibly happy if they save her boy, Penn. They live nearby in a cottage along with their large extended family. The family's gratitude can be expressed through the sharing of food, beds, and information about the area and the dangers that lay ahead.

The patriarch of the family gives them a jug of his home-brewed Birch Root Gin. It is powerfully intoxicating and also useful as a stain remover.

Puzzling Tome

SUMMARY: They find a valuable book locked inside a mechanical puzzle.

READ TO THE PLAYERS

A glint of metal catches the eye leading you to an ornate contraption laying on the ground. Upon further inspection, it appears to be a book, but one that is locked within a very complicated apparatus. The leather and brass mechanism is covered in a tangle of gears, dials, and levers. Scratches and dents indicate that someone spent considerable effort trying to open the book before succumbing to frustration and discarding it. This is a puzzle-lock and there is only one solution.

Present the illustration on the opposite page to your players.

Three ways to open:

Notes: Neither the mechanism nor the book are magical. You should only allow another character to Aid in a check if they are also proficient in that skill or tool.

INT(tinker's tools) DC 20: Using their understanding of mechanisms, they can more easily solve the puzzle lock. Each attempt takes half an hour.

INT(thieves tools) DC 21: Using thieves tools, they can try to bypass some of the mechanisms and trick the apparatus into opening. Each attempt takes half an hour.

INT(investigation) DC 22: Using pure brain power and concentration, a smart person can figure out the puzzle, eventually. Each attempt takes 1 hour.

TREASURE & RESOLUTION

When finally revealed, the treasured tome turns out to be a lengthy dissertation on a useful topic.
- The book should ideally be written in a language only one or two of your players know.
- Once studied, understood, and practiced, the knowledge in the tome gives a character proficiency in a skill, tool, weapon, kit, or saving throw. You must decide what proficiency the tome is written about.
- A character must study the book for at least 14 hours per week. At the end of each week they may make an Intelligence check with a bonus of +1 for each week they have been studying. Once they achieve a DC 30, they gain the proficiency and no longer need the tome.

HELD IN SILKEN SLUMBER

SUMMARY: An encounter with giant spiders takes an unexpected turn when a cocooned manticore breaks free.

CR1 500 xp 1 Giant Spider	
CR2 900 xp 2 Giant Spiders	
CR3 1200 xp 3 Giant Spiders	
CR4 1500 xp 4 Giant Spiders	
CR5 2800 xp 8 Giant Spiders	

READ TO THE PLAYERS

The trees here are very tall and dripping with ropes of old spider webs. High above, in every direction, you can see vast webs stretching between the soaring branches. You have no doubt that giant spiders are lurking up there.

> Pause to allow the players to react to the scene, readying weapons or shields, for example.

As anticipated, an enormous spider drops upon you from above, spinning a silken strand as is descends.

GIANT SPIDER CR 1 (200xp)
Large monstrosity, lawful evil

Armor Class 14 (natural armor)
Hit Points 26 (4d10+4) **Speed** 30 ft., climb 30 ft.

STR	DEX	CON	INT	WIS	CHA
14 (+2)	16 (+3)	12 (+1)	2 (-4)	11 (+0)	4 (-3)

Skills Stealth +7, Perception +3
Senses Darkvision 60 ft., passive Perception 13
Languages –

Spider Traits: The spider can climb difficult surfaces without making a check. It knows the location and distance to any creature touching its web. It ignores movement restrictions caused by webs.

ACTIONS
Bite. Melee Weapon Attack: +5 to hit, reach 5ft., one target, Hit: 7 (1d8+3) piercing damage, and target must make a DC 11 Constitution saving throw, taking 2d8 poison damage on a failed save or 1d8 on a successful one. A creature reduced to 0 hitpoints by poison is paralyzed but not killed and regains hitpoints normally.

Web. Ranged Weapon Attack: +5 to hit, range 30/60 ft., one target, Hit: Target is restrained. DC 12 Strength check to break free. Webbing has AC 10; hp 5 and vulnerable to fire but immune to bludgeoning.

COMBAT

Round 1: The giant spider makes a bite attack at whomever looks least armored. Two more spiders, if the CR allows, drop down from above.

Round 2: One spider makes a web attack while any others make bite attacks. They will spread out their attacks among all targets. Two more spiders, if the CR allows, drop down from above.

Round 3: One spider makes a web attack while any others make bite attacks. A large cocoon is shaken loose from the webs above and crashes to the ground in the midst of the melee. Whomever is there must make a DC 11 Dexterity saving throw or suffer 2d6 bludgeoning damage.

Round 4: Whatever spiders are there all make web attacks and any remaining spiders listed in the CR drop down this round. The cocooned creature begins thrashing around and tearing free of its cocoon with long claws.

Round 5: All the spiders make bite attacks. The manticore shakes off the last of the webbing. It is injured. Its left arm and left wing are both broken so it cannot fly away. Angry and confused, it will attack randomly at whomever is closest, PC or spider, using either bite and claw, or throwing tail spikes if no one is adjacent.

Rounds 6+: The chaotic melee continues. The spiders want to capture PCs to eat. The manticore wants to kill everyone or at least drive them away.

INJURED MANTICORE CR 2 (450xp)
Large monstrosity, lawful evil

Armor Class 14 (natural armor)
Hit Points 34 (8d10+24) **Speed** 30 ft.

STR	DEX	CON	INT	WIS	CHA
16 (+3)	15 (+2)	16 (+3)	7 (-2)	12 (+1)	8 (-1)

Senses Darkvision 60 ft., passive Perception 11
Languages Common

Tail Spike Regrowth. The manticore has twenty-four tail spikes which regrow during a long rest.

ACTIONS

Multiattack The manticore makes two attacks: one with its bite and one with its unbroken arm or two with its tail spikes.

Bite. Melee Weapon Attack: +5 to hit, reach 5ft., one target, Hit: 7 (1d8+3) piercing damage.

Claw. Melee Weapon Attack: +5 to hit, reach 5ft., one target, Hit: 6 (1d6+3) slashing damage.

Tail Spike. Ranged Weapon Attack: +5 to hit, range 100/200 ft., one target, Hit: 7 (1d8+3) piercing damage.

WALL BALL, ANYONE?

SUMMARY: The party is invited to join in a friendly game of sport.

READ TO THE PLAYERS

Up ahead is a monastery. Joyful noises draw your attention to the abbey's south wall where a group of friars are playing a game, pitching a ball off the wall and then running to catch it. Upon seeing you, one of the men jogs over to the road to talk with you.

"Greetings, travelers! You wouldn't fancy a bit of sport, would you? We invented this game we call Wall Ball, but we haven't enough players to make it really fun."

Two Teams:

The friars have a number of players equal to the size of the adventuring party. They form one team and the PCs form the opposing team.

Rules of the game:

A gravel path curves around the abbey. This curve divides the grassy playing field into two areas, the infield and the outfield. The ball is made of tightly wound twine coated in wax.

Each player will take turns as the pitcher, getting four throws. They bounce the ball off the wall and into the outfield. If the ball reaches the outfield and isn't caught by an opponent, a point is scored. After four throws, the other team mans the outfield. The game is over once everyone has pitched.

Game mechanics:

The pitcher will make a STR(athletics) check to throw the ball against the wall. This check sets the DC for the catchers. If the check is below 8, the ball does not make it past the gravel path.

Roll randomly to see which outfielder the ball will land closest to. That catcher makes a DEX(acrobatics) check. If they meet the DC set by the pitcher, the ball is caught.

The friars have a +4 bonus to their athletics checks and acrobatics checks.

Betting on the second game:

So long as they weren't humiliated in the first game, the friars will be willing to bet money on a second game, up to five gold per man.

Names for the friars:

Wenlo, Pemrash, Ragane, Epidyn, Deldan, Drook, Scarmack, Galsh, Logopher

TREASURE & RESOLUTION

Win or lose, the friars are just happy they had the chance to play their new game to its fullest. They will offer the party as much hospitality as they can. They can provide a meal and beds. As studious men, they may have important information about the players' current quest.

Wall of Heroes

David Bonney

Kevin Dolan

Jeffrey Ober

Josh van Lier

Christiano Pagani

F. Kirkpatrick

With gratitude to all the intrepid adventurers who supported this project and followed me into the unknown.

Call To Adventure
Expanded Compendium of Fifth Edition Backgrounds

The classic Hero's Journey begins with humble beginnings. This meek and predictable life is what makes the next step, the call to adventure, so terrifying. The 13 backgrounds presented in D&D's Player's Handbook covered a lot of possible backstories, but the sense of humble beginnings was missing. What if there were another thirty or more backgrounds to choose from? What if each one had a uniqueness that added flavor and personality to your player character? What if your background wasn't the thing you chose at the end of your character design, but was the life you were Called To Adventure from?

Available at Amazon.com in hardcover and paperback

CPSIA information can be obtained
at www.ICGtesting.com
Printed in the USA
LVHW072309311021
702040LV00004B/70